"Chuck Meyer writes like Tom Robbins, Garrison Keillor and John Irving combined." Martha Meyer, *Age 86* ("Who are those people? He made me say that. Put that rubber hose away, son...AAAAIIIIIEEEEE.")

"I'm 88 years old and I like this book because the print is big enough to read." Carl F. Meyer, Sr. ("Was that okay? Can we come live with you now?")

"Fun and nostalgic for those of us over forty. Good preparation for those approaching it. Required reading for anyone in the throes." Lt. Col. Carl F. Meyer, Jr. ("Get my name right on the check, little brother.")

"My husband pours himself into every story. Doomed to be a bestseller." Debi Meyer ("Something in a Lexus would be nice.")

"It's wonderful that someone Dad's age can still write; and with less hair, too." Michal Meyer ("Now does my allowance go up?")

"Great litter-ary material. Shred this book." Murphy Meyer. Cat.

Also by Chuck Meyer

SURVIVING DEATH: A PRACTICAL GUIDE TO CARING FOR THE
DYING AND BEREAVED

GOD'S LAUGHTER AND OTHER HERESIES

THE EIGHTH DAY, LETTERS, POEMS AND PARABLES

THE GOSPEL ACCORDING TO BUBBA

FAST funny AND 40

STONE ANGEL BOOKS
AUSTIN, TEXAS

Printed in the United States of America at Morgan Printing in
Austin, Texas.

ISBN #0-9631149-3-X

For
Larry Bugen
friend
fellow struggler
and unindicted co-conspirator
on the journey

PROLOGUE

It began with a haircut I couldn't get.

The detour through hair hell and back to my normal red-and-white-striped barber shop alerted me to my view of the world through the squinting (soon to be bifocaled) eyes of my forties. I began to notice that each experience I had - even though it was something familiar that I had done for decades - was somehow different than it had been a few short years ago. Whether it had to do with buying a car, raising my daughter, dealing with parents, or exercising - something strange was occurring that called for reflection and comment. Events and tasks were the same, but the perspective and feelings were now surprisingly different.

The stories burst forth before me one at a time like novas, bright starbursts, over the course of a few years. (That's why my daughter's age ranges from ten to thirteen, depending on the topic.) As the searing light from them illumined parts of myself and my family that I had not seen quite in these ways before, I shared the shiny new "forties-stories" with close friends. In doing so I learned that they too were dealing with the same issues in similar ways and our mutual stories seemed to shed a helpful light on each other's lives.

One person suggested the sub-title "Male-tales of Mid-life" because they are, of course, written from a man's point of view. But women who read them laughed more then their male counterparts, perhaps more objectively appreciating the jokes.

Eventually, the nova-stories combined to form this book. Light reading.

The title is three-dimensional. The tales themselves are quickly read, mostly funny, and all about life in our forties. Likewise, our fourth decade seems to pass far too fast, revealing parts of ourselves that can only be survived if we see the humor in them. And my wife and daughter think that because I run and write stories (not at the same time), the title fits for me as well.

On the incredible assumption that you haven't read my other books, it will be helpful in understanding these pieces to know that I was born (1947 Boomer) and raised in Cincinnati, Ohio, received degrees from various places in Indiana, New York and Connecticut, and all of my graduate education from the inmates and staff of a New York prison and a Texas jail. After ten years in prison chaplaincy I went on to post-graduate learning from the patients, families and staff of St. David's Hospital in Austin, Texas. There I continue to witness the intricacies of Ben Casey's intro: man, woman, life, death, infinity, with the emphasis on death, dying, and grief. I hold forth there as Director of Pastoral Care and Assistant Vice President of Patient Relations.

The rest is in the stories.

Special thanks are due to my wife Debi, and freelancer Rhonda Cloos, both writers who are good editors, wielding red pens like blackjacks. Special apologies are due my daughter, who provides me with great joy, constant hair jokes (because mine is "thinning,") and multiple occasions for thinking about my aging - many of which are included here, much to her chagrin.

These tales represent only a few issues of our forties. Others will present themselves and will have to be told. Perhaps it is only in our forties that we begin to appreciate the power of our individual and combined stories to help us sort through the debris we have accumulated in four decades of living. Perhaps it is only by our forties that we have the perspective not to take either the issues or ourselves with terminal seriousity.

In fact, it is only in the telling of our tales to one another, hanging them out on our communal backyard clothesline to air in the cleansing daylight of each other's critique and support, that we gain the strength, perspective, and, most importantly, the humor required both to endure and enjoy the journey.

It is my hope that, if we tell our stories together, we will reach the next decade of our lives with an attitude that will take us through those years and beyond - well forty-fied.

Austin, Texas
August, 1994

TALES

CARS
1

DAUGHTER
20

GOD
33

U-TROU
45

SHAVING
57

SANDWICH
69

MASSAGE
83

HAIRCUT
109

A GOOD DEATH
124

EXERCISE
140

EPILOGUE
154

ix

CARS

The first car I remember was a 1936 Chevrolet.

If you do your addition you will wonder how it is that I can be in my forties and remember a car that old. It is because I was raised by Depression Era parents of the Germanic persuasion, a combination resulting in permanent sphincter closure. They keep scraps of paper forever and stockpile everything else in closets because you never can tell when you'll need something and when you do it is certain you'll never have enough. To this day, if there is any kind of national disaster, my parents will be armed with enough toilet paper in the basement to last them - and the neighborhood - for years. Acquired on sale of course.

Thus the 1936 Chevrolet lasted until 1951, and my father (recently turned 88) *still* regrets parting with it, imagining the car to be traveling down an obscure country road with somebody "still getting some use out of it."

The car was green, kind of a lime green actually, very unusual in an era when cars were either black or dark blue because you never knew when some

aberrant kamikaze would be flying over, looking for
light colored automobiles to destroy to conquer Cincinnati for Hirohito. I always wondered what pos-
sessed my Dad to buy a green one. He would just
have turned 30 and, if my relative's memories are
accurate, was full of piss and vinegar at the time, so
that probably had something to do with it.

I remember the wide, black running boards along
both sides, where my friends and I played gangsters,
rocking our green Elliot Ness car and hanging on
the door handles, shooting at Capone and Baby Face
Nelson as we rounded the imaginary curve on two
huge wheels.

The back seat was so big you felt like you were
riding in a train car. There were no seat belts, of
course, or turn signals for that matter. In a car that
surrounded you with that much steel you could
afford to be a little cavalier about what got in your
way.

I was five when we bought the '51 Chevy. The
thing that most impressed me in the purchase was
not the shiny newness of the car or its considerable
smallness after the Pullman we'd all enjoyed, but
the fact that my father thought we hadn't waited
nearly long enough to trade in the '36. He had only
driven that car a mere *fifteen* years, and it was "hardly
broke in."

My own philosophy of cars has, at least up until
now, been that of my family. It still amazes me
("horrifies" is more accurate) to learn in my forties

how much I have carried over from my parents. It is difficult to admit that these tendencies which once were rejected, despised and thought stupid, have now, like some subversive genetic implant, become the guiding principles for such serious life decisions as car buying, among other things.

I once owned a used '71 Toyota Corolla 1200 and drove it until the odometer registered 4500 miles for the second time. There was something extraordinarily satisfying about watching those little digits slip, one by one, over the 100,000 mark. It is gratifying, at least to those of us raised by Depression Era parents, to know that we have truly gotten the most out of the automobile, that we have used it to its full purpose, that we have purchased well, maintained carefully, and above all *not wasted* money by trading it in before it was *absolutely necessary*. Some people even calculate the cost per mile and satisfy themselves by figuring out they actually spent, say fifty-five cents every time they got behind the wheel. The Depression Era parents of those people can be particularly proud.

As they used to say in the summaries of the PSAT and SAT study tests, the key words in the above description are *wasted* and *necessary*. It is as if we were taught that there is Someone, somewhere, keeping track of every automobile purchased by the adult children of Depression Era parents. Records are maintained by that Someone to assure to those parents (dead or alive) that everything possible was done to sustain the life of the child's car before it was traded in on a new one, that no superfluous purchases were made, and that the replacement vehicle will outlast the old by ten years or so given the newer technology. Only then can the adult child sleep at night without worrying about the unnecessary waste of money in the garage. Perhaps we need a Twelve Step Program for Adult Children of Depression Era Parents, except that we would have to complete it in Ten.

The only thing better than driving a car forever was to drive one for free. That's how we got the "wienermobile."

My father worked for the Kahn's Meat Packing Company in Cincinnati, Ohio, which in 1962 was a major rival of Oscar Mayer. As the Director of Public Relations he was constantly bringing home volumes of Kahn's wiener key chains, wiener refrigerator magnets, wristwatches with wiener second hands, wiener beanies, wiener napkins and wiener decals. Needless to say, these items made me quite popular with other junior high kids who gladly accepted these trinkets and proceeded to do obscene things with them that none of us quite understood yet.

One summer evening my father appeared in the kitchen with a proud grin on his face and pointed to the back door.

"Go see what the Company bought me." He always referred to the Company like it was the CIA. I kept expecting him to bring home exploding wieners.

My mother and brother and I looked out in the driveway and saw a bright yellow 1962 Plymouth *with a huge wiener on the top.* This wiener was the entire length of the car. Bolted permanently to the roof, it would not fit under the metal bar in parking garages. It tilted up on both ends, like a wiener. It was brown, like a wiener, except for the red and yellow wrapper in the center on which the company slogan was emblazoned in letters a bat could read at two hundred yards. The slogan was (and still *is*): "THE WIENER THE WORLD AWAITED." (I am NOT making this up.)

I anticipated a frenzy of laughter when my Dad dropped me off in front of school the next morning. To my surprise there were two reactions. The dorky kids thought it was dorky and made crude jokes which I shall leave to the imagination. But the popular kids with whom I was desperately trying to identify actually thought it was, in the vernacular of the day, "neat."

My stock went up. Kids fought for the privilege of letting Mr. Meyer drive them home from the "hop" in the Kahn's Wiener Car, which always had greasy windows and smelled like lunch meat. They begged me to ask him to drive it to parties. I was elected Student Council President and had my chubby, dorky eighth grade picture on the cover of the Graduation Dance pamphlet. Girls, however, did not fall all over me, nor did their fathers encourage them to date me, horrified at the prospect of watching their precious young daughters get into a car proclaiming that this boy actually had some connection with THE WIENER THE WORLD AWAITED.

I do not know whatever happened to the wiener car, but I suspect it was taken off the road when food warning labels were mandated.

So it was that my inherited car genes zoomed along pedal to the metal sans seat belts or turn signals and I approached my mid-forties in an '85 Honda Prelude nearing the 100,000 mile mark. I had driven that car for nine years with great satisfaction, having done the scheduled maintenance and babied it through 98000 miles with no major difficulties. But somewhere in the last forty six years there had been a recessive gene rebellion inside me that wanted something new before the old thing had completely been worn down to nothing (after which you gave it to Goodwill and took a tax deduction.)

Besides, this was mid-life and everybody I knew was either having affairs or buying cars. Fortunately I am happily married to a wonderful wife with a charming daughter and a tolerable cat, so the affair was out. Besides, if I had an affair they would bludgeon me with a well-deserved ballbat, Barbie, and yarn ball, claim total insanity and enjoy the insurance money. So I went for the car.

Cautiously, so as not to attract the attention of the Someone watching my mileage and money, I secretly perused the Automotive Section of the Sunday paper. I also began to pay more attention to the other cars on the road, imagining myself in a new Prelude, Celica or Mazda MX6, or even a Miata. Noticing no ill effects from this surreptitious exercise, I took one step further - I started going to car dealerships on weekends, just to *look* of course.

It was a difficult task, this looking for a replacement car for the one I had been attached to for so long, had known so well and had, like my father before me, barely broken in. At first I found myself looking for an exact duplicate. I wanted the trunk lines to be the same, the interior to be the same, the flip up headlights to be the same. If only I could have magically found a mint 1985 Honda Prelude in some Depression Era spinster's garage up on blocks, bought at the time like the extra box of on-sale detergent, ready in case another Depression occurred and she needed a car.

But no, there was to be no exact duplicate of my wonderful old car. There were other cars with the same name, but the model design had changed. Gone were the classic lines, the clean cut angles, the clear and easy view from all sides. Instead I found cars that looked as though they were designed for long legged midgets with x-ray vision and no friends. The bodies were like a pig in a boa constrictor, flat on both ends and humped in the middle. You couldn't see the trunk from either the rear view mirror or even by looking over your right shoulder, so you had to take it on faith that it was there and guess where it was heading when you backed up. There was *no* back seat, though the engineers had managed to devise an optical illusion that made you *think* there was a back seat. If you had friends or children larger than a chihuahua they would have to take the bus. These non-back-seats all folded down, of course, allowing you arm length access to the trunk, where your kids were lying strapped to the floor.

There were always *two* front seats, but only a *driver's* side air bag. One can only imagine that the engineers thought the survival of the spouse, friend or s.o. was not a requirement for the continued happiness of the maniac behind the wheel.

These new cars were all rounded, supposedly more aerodynamic and fuel efficient (except when you read the negative MPG on the label.) But this "roundness" made them all look like a fetal version of the '49 Hudson, which my Dad called "an inverted bathtub on wheels." Hudson embryos.

I was depressed at the dearth of prospects. I wanted the right car in which to *ride out my forties.* Indeed, the way I take care of cars this would be the one in which I would ride out the *century.* Suddenly the purchase took on much greater significance. This car had to make a statement about *both* of those issues. Perhaps that is the plague of being in our forties. We are past the point of purchasing merely for basic transportation (as we did in our twenties,) or for family belongings (as in our thirties.) Now we want something to reward

ourselves for having sacrificed in the past, along
with something that will securely drive us into the
future in relative comfort (one hesitates to say
"luxury," though that is part of the picture).

In addition, our forties allow us to *see* into the
future and force us to start thinking retirement
thoughts, along with AARP aging thoughts, along
with declining physical ability thoughts - so this purchase suddenly becomes the car that drives me out
of my forties, out of this decade, out of this century
and *out of middle age* into my fifties. This was becoming a *significant decision.*

As I searched for the car to meet these emotional
requirements, it became clear that the young, yuppie
designers who produced these baby Hudsons thought
that people my age wouldn't be buying them anyway, so why design them for us? But one of the
things we know in our forties that our younger counterparts have not yet figured out is that persistence
pays off. So I was determined to find the exact car
that would satisfy me and my genes.

I quickly learned that, though the cars had certainly changed in nine years, the salespersons hadn't.
Nobody goes directly from high school into new car
sales. It would be better if they did. The introduction
story would be shorter.

"Hi. I'm Freddie Jones. I graduated High
School in 1965 and been working here ever
since."

Now there's a salesperson you can trust. He's got a history with cars, knows every model the company ever put out. You can count on him to be there forever, he loves it so much, and that inspires confidence in the dealership.

Of course Freddie Jones does not exist, probably by Federal law written by the National Car Dealers Association. Instead, every salesperson is a former something else, and the other part of the Federal Car Dealers Law is that the person must *tell* you their entire personal life story leading up to this obviously inferior job in car sales before you can get down to the actual purpose of your visit to the dealership, which, if you remember, was to purchase a car, or as many of the salespeople call it - "a vehicle." You know the person's previous life involved some contact with the military if they keep using the term "the vehicle" when referring to the car you'd like to test drive if only they would come up for air.

But first the life story, usually involving unforseen tragedy and epic misfortune that would shame the soaps.

"Hi, I'm Robert Hutchinson. And *you* are...?"

"Chuck Mey..."

"Glad to meet you Chuck. You know, I wasn't always in this business."

"No kidd..."

"It all started when my Daddy died at age four."

"Your father was four when he di..?"

"It was very sad. I had to be the man of the house. You know what I mean, Chuck?"

"Well, about this ca..."

"So I just jumped right in and raised my eight brothers and sisters single handed, until that little mishap with the police when my mother got shot and paralyzed from the neck down. I was working three jobs - none of them in car sales, you understand - and going to school at night. Had to feed her like a baby, Chuck."

"Would you like a Kleenex?"

"Thanks, I'll just use your hanky here." Snort. "So I joined the Marines to go fight in 'Nam. That's the reason for this little limp you might have noticed. Nothing big, really. Just picked up some shrapnel while rescuing a buddy. Carried his body fourteen miles through enemy fire before the choppers picked us up. Course he was dead by that time, but did I know?" Snort. "Then nobody would hire me when I returned Stateside, with the limp and all, and I admit I was a little crazy then, drugs and booze, you know what I mean, Chuck? So I worked odd jobs for a few years till I found my niche in vacuum cleaners." Grin. "Now there's a job that really sucks." Wink. "Get it, Chuck?"

"What colors exactly...does this car...?"

"That's where I met my first ex-wife, Geraldine. Her daddy owned the place, so after the divorce and the murder trial I went through another long series of employment opportunities, as they say. After my second divorce and the bypass surgery I had to take it slow, so that's how I got here in this business where I can take my good old time getting to know customers like you, Buck."

"Chuck."

"Right. Now let me tell you about these cars. I used to work for the other guys South of town but they are so slimy I said to myself, I said, 'Self, these guys are too slimy even for you, so we're *outta* here.' And I came up to this dealership where they are ethical and forthright and honest to a fault."

"How much does...?"

"We can work any deal you want, Muck. I'll work it for you personally. The Sales Manager is a personal friend of mine. We go dove hunting every September and I haven't hit him yet." Laugh. "So you just put together the package you want and I'll take it to him and we'll work the best deal you've ever gotten, Suck."

There seemed to be two kinds of dealerships. The first kind had salespeople all dressed in the same color and style of short sleeved shirt with the dealer logo scripted over the left chest. These people were neatly dressed with regulation haircuts, khaki pants and shined shoes. They exuded professionalism and confidence and a sense that you would pay a higher price but it would be worth it because they had to pay the janitor to keep the place spotless and the barbers to keep their hair neat.

The other kind of dealership had balloons on the radio antennas, a little booth giving away free already popped and re-heated popcorn, flat soft drinks, bright red hot dogs (not Kahn's), and matted cotton candy - always a hit with the kids before test driving a new car. The salespeople here reached new heights of heterogeneity, both of attire and tonsorial unkemptness. These folks had clashing polyester shirts and pants, unpolished and scuffed shoes, hair that reeked of Brylcream or hairspray, and a clear mandate to deal with as many customers as possible as fast as possible with as little explanation as possible, except for their personal life story of tragedy.

Out of curiosity (and competitive shopping) my wife and I wandered into one of these places. Between the shouting over the loud speaker for sales*men* (some of whom were women) to come to the desk for a customer, and the hard rock music blaring heavy metal because someone thought it appropriate for *cars* ("Get it, Cluck?"), our senses were reduced to a flat line on the monitor. We sat in the glass walled, reverberating office of a saleswoman wearing a dress from Omar the Tentmaker, under which she probably hid two or three vehicles for her personal use. She had a big picture of her dog and a smaller one of her husband prominently displayed near the phone and knick knacks everywhere on her desk, including a cutesy orange gourd with a happy face on it and "Happy Thanksgiving" spelled out in little wooden letter blocks. She rather insolently refused to give us a bottom line price, repeatedly thrust credit applications under our noses, and then left the room, purportedly to converse with her credit manager, but actually, we thought, to phone her dog. While she was gone we rearranged the little wooden blocks to say "I THINK U GAGS" which was kinder than "SAGG" which was *my* first preference, and then we left.

It is clear that car dealers are not equipped to deal with those of us in our forties. We are largely products of the Sixties where we learned to "QUESTION AUTHORITY" at every turn. We are used to getting what we want and we suffer no foolish excuses such as "I don't have that model with that equipment in stock" to which we angrily reply: "SO CAN'T YOU *GET* IT?"

We are not the docile, unquestioning, passive patrons that can be run roughshod over, even though we (or I at least) always feel taken for a ride when going through this exercise of lies, games and deception, values that we thought SDS had extinguished in the Sixties. So it gave me great satisfaction to *walk* on a deal.

I had signed a contract to buy a car and told the saleswoman (not the previous, corpulent one) I had financing arranged. She, with a twenty five minute personal life tragedy story and no ears, indicated I needed to talk with their finance manager. I again explained that I had financing arranged. She led me to his office. He tried to sell me a loan. I declined politely the first time. The second time I declined less politely. When he insinuated I was making a "stupid mistake" by not financing with them I walked back to the saleswoman and tore up the contract, stating that I could not do business "with any dealership that would employ an asshole like that." I did not indicate what kind of asshole I *would* do business with.

With a bow to the genetic information implanted in my bones, I learned later that my father had done the same thing over some snide comment from a salesman about an "oil pan," whatever that is, under the car. Dad got great satisfaction out of recalling the tale and I got depressed thinking that my genes were dragging me into late adulthood toward the model sitting across the table.

The more I searched the more I hated the game. It seems that, when you turn forty - and *certainly* forty-five - you should be beyond all this. The scenario would go something like this:

"Hello, I'm Jack Winsten."

"I'm Chuck Meyer and I want to know about that car there."

"That car there will cost you exactly $18,500 fully equipped and not a penny more or less and you can go to any other dealer in this state and the price will be the same just as if you went to another supermarket and bought skim milk."

"I'll take it."

"Sign here."

No life stories on either side. I do not want to know this person or want him to know me. I am not beginning an intimate friendship here, I am buying a car. I hate the stupid gaming and posturing and seeing who can outscrew whom on the deal. And by my forties I should not be required to *do* this any more.

Then the impossible happened. I finally found a car I actually liked enough to buy. Unfortunately this event came at the very time when, after inspecting every automobile known to mankind and dealing with various insufferable car salespersons of every width, hair style and previous employment record imaginable, I had decided to obey my genes, *keep* my old car and drive it until one of us was permanently unroadworthy.

The salesman, after the obligatory tragic story involving war wounds and football injuries, gave me the "bottom line price." I said I'd have to check it with the buying service from AAA, bring that price back and he'd have to check with his Sales Manager (the fictitious character in the little nonexistent room upstairs who allegedly "approves" all sales), and then I'd have to check it with the Pope and the Archbishop of Canterbury and Hannibal Lector and Willy Nelson and then we'd get back with each other and haggle some more. We agreed to meet in a few days, and I figured I would just not call him back. If I stalled long enough, the urge would diminish and would be overtaken by my desire to keep my wonderful old car.

Fortunately for the salesman, who by now was on his third divorce, his second "athletic injury", and his eighteenth job, I was intruded upon by grace, by unsolicited and unwanted manna from heaven, in the form of a phone call from my sister-in-law who told me that she had found someone who would buy my old car at the full price I wanted so there would be no haggling about that little detail from the fictitious Sales Manager.

Push came to shove when the buyer handed me a check. There were no more excuses. Like the lyrics of a country/western song, I stood in the driveway watching my precious old car drive off in the hands of a stranger. It was then that the real issue hit home like a punch from Ali.

Change.

There, in one grey package on four wheels, went nine years of my life. The car stood for the transition from my thirties to my forties, from singlehood to married with child and cat. I had grown comfortable with my identity in that automobile. I knew how the clutch felt, had the gear ratios down to a precise art, judged the cornering perfectly, had become one with the hum of the engine like a Buddhist with Om. I knew who I was in that car, both at work and at home. Seeing that identity drive down the street without me left me feeling lonely, uncertain, empty, facing the rest of my forties without the familiarity of the past. I was being forced to move forward, not just with the new technology of a new automobile, but with the new person, the older person, the late forties person who stood in the driveway watching.

But I also began to experience a sense of adventure in saying goodbye to the past nine years; a sense of curiosity about where the new car would take me, who we would become together, how our identities would grow through the remainder of my forties and - reality strikes again - into my fifties.

It occurred to me that that is what our forties are about in a way that other decades of our lives are not - the change from the immediacy of youth, that constant search for instant gratification and the hurry to grow and progress, to the slower paced life brought on by a beginning sense of perspective. In our forties we have the ability both to look back *and* to look forward with equally reasonable vision, at least until we need bifocals. We can get stuck holding onto the identity of the past if we are unaware that growth and change are the natural order of things, and that there are equally interesting and exciting things ahead as those we have accomplished comfortably behind us.

The next day I purchased a Celica GT. But I went to a different dealership in a small town and found a kid just out of high school who called me "Sir" and just wanted to sell cars.

I did have to hear about his girlfriend.

Buying a new car in your forties is risky. Not to buy one is even riskier.

Maybe that's why Dad got the green one.

DAUGHTER

My daughter's name is Michal Leah.

I love her.

I did not have kids in my first marriage. My wife and I, in our twenties and early thirties, were perfectly content with each other, did not want the responsibility or the intrusiveness of a third party (human or animal), and basically spent all of our time together luxuriating in the pleasure of our own company. Having been the primary caregiver for her (thirteen years younger) sister growing up, my wife claimed she did not need a child to fulfill her life; she thoroughly enjoyed her work and filled her leisure time with projects and mutually agreeable activities.

I hadn't given the idea of children much thought when I got married. I must have assumed they were the logical consequence of unprotected sex, much as AIDS and STDs are today, and that, like these latter disasters, they were to be tolerated dolefully and addressed dutifully, much as my brother and I were. I was content, therefore, tacitly to comply with the decision to live a birth-controlled "child-free" life and

20

came to take for granted the ability to spend whole evenings reading or writing, to spontaneously lock up the house and take off together for a weekend or longer, and to begin to accumulate savings for present play and future security.

When my wife suddenly died, my entire identity was called into question at the very vulnerable age of thirty-four. As I gradually emerged from the cocoon of grief, I developed criteria for "finding someone" and spent the next six years dating only single women with no kids, fully and foolishly expecting to find someone with whom to repeat the previous experience of nearly total symbiosis. After six years of experience, I came to the conclusion that I would never marry again and had satisfactorily accepted this fact. I became comfortable, even content, with my single lifestyle, ready to live it out that way to the end.

Just when I had it all figured it out, I met a woman who was in a similar situation - quite comfortable with her independent single status, with little thought to changing it, ever. We were immediately, though with some understandable reluctance and trepidation, attracted to each other and, knowing how short life is, in six months found ourselves walking down a church aisle together.

Along with her came a six-year-old girl child and two cats.

The cats were easier to handle.

Like any other person who is thrown headlong

into the purgatory of parenthood, there was no way to prepare for the time constraints and emotional demands this small human being required.

In my single life, my non-work hours were spent almost entirely at my own whim; I could come home or not, eat in or out, write all night till I fell asleep at the computer or read and awake in my leather lounge chair, fly to New York to an exhibition and to visit friends, or hole up and not answer the phone for the entire weekend. I was also terribly and overwhelmingly alone, without the joy of companionship in things small and large.

Marriage wonderfully solved the problem of companionship. A daughter solved the problem of being alone. I had not anticipated the daily chores of lacing and tying various things on a little person, listening to complex commentaries on everything from school to playmates, answering questions on easy things such as why there is war and what to do about werewolves, and hard things like whether or not there is a Santa Claus and is the Easter Bunny a girl? I had not known about monitoring the t.v., patience with homework, 2 a.m. nightmares, inextricable (and inexplicable) morning tangles in angel-fine hair, or emergency room visits for gashed appendages.

In all fairness, I must admit I lucked out. This child was so sweet that I nearly needed insulin. Her divorced mother had done an incredible job of raising her solo for six years, and imparting her own qualities of kindness, respect, compassion, empathy, good sense, and playfulness that so attracted me in the first place.

That was the good news.

The bad news was that my relatively stable and basically unexamined life of unquestioned narcissism was now open to the relentless, unending and totally dedicated scrutiny of a child. I mean, what else have they to do?

In fact it seemed that, just as I was making constant erudite comments on everything she did and did not do, instructing and cajoling and reprimanding and supporting in my newly-expert know-it-all parent way, she was doing the same back to me.

I was trapped. I began to resent all the syrupy advice my friends (especially psychologists) had given me when confronted with my arguments about marrying someone with kids. Of course they *all* had kids. In fact they had what Zorba the Greek called "the full catastrophe" - wife, kids, house - and I secretly wondered if their misty eyed monologues about the inexorable joys of parenthood had not been meant to lure me into their common misery, lest I escape the tribulation they continued to endure at the sticky hands of their ungrateful children.

I began to think Plato was horribly wrong. The unexamined life that I had heretofore known was not only worth living, it was highly desireable in contrast to a life innocently regurgitated back in the mouthy mirror of a six-year-old girl.

To my amazement, it seemed that her journey

through kidhood kept raising issues that had somehow gone unnoticed by me in my twenties and early thirties. Conversations and experiences with her sent me immediately to my laptop to reflect on the wisdom of her simple comments or the deeper implications of her actions. Where I started out thinking I, as parent, would be the primary teacher to her inexperienced absorbent mind, I quickly found myself learning equally from her about life, about herself and, painfully, about myself.

As she struggled with failures, friendships, her place in the new world of our new family, bad and good dreams, successes, disappointments, shots and stitches, State capitols, school plays, death of a family friend, sleep overs, dance recitals, and homework - so did I.

As I struggled with failures, friendships, my place in the new world of our new family with her and her mother, finding a literary agent, book and story rejects, tighter budget constraints, distant aging parents, the daily life and death stories of hospital and personal life - so did she.

As the three of us struggled together (five if you include the cats Maxie and Sugar) she became the primary focus of reflective stories I wrote for publication - and they became a book called "GOD'S LAUGHTER - AND OTHER HERESIES." They chronicle our metamorphoses: hers from an only child of a single mother to a family member who must negotiate for time and attention; mine from an introverted widower who never wanted children to a married man with a ubiquitous daughter. Neither of us would be the same without the other's influence. We are, each of us, indelibly marked.

But maybe that is what children are for. I have come to believe propagation of the species is secondary, and that the *function* of kids is to force adults - parents and others to whom parents brag and complain - to deal with issues we would rather avoid, pass through unnoticed, or comfortably rationalize into our carefully structured and well defended worldview. As we watch them go through the things we did at their age we are reminded of how we did it, what it meant, how our own parents reacted to us. Layers of packed emotional sediment, like paint in the bottom of a can in our mind's garage, forgotten sludge from the deepest recesses of our psyche is suddenly prodded, stirred into consciousness by the inadvertent poking of our kids.

Like whirling flakes of mud in an old Coke bottle your child dug out of your psychological stream bed, the issues are raised again - only this time they are spinning in full view of everyone: yourself, your spouse, your kid, and everyone in the supermarket, the PTA, and the church service watching you deal with them.

So the opportunity is there to review those issues from the perspective of an (alleged) adult, to finish unfinished business, to forgive and be forgiven, and, most importantly, to make sure we perpetuate the syndrome by foisting the same psychoses on our own children for raising the issues in the first place.

I am certain I have made mistakes with my daughter, enough to guarantee a lifetime of income to some psychologist, or series of psychologists in her future. A friend of mine has a "Shrink Kitty" in the kitchen. Every time he makes a mistake with his kid he puts a dollar in the kitty to pay for the future work that will need to be done to undo the damage.

There was the time I thought she would like a giant, three dimensional, lifelike E.T. poster. So I put it on her bathroom mirror and awoke to her shrieks at two in the morning when she'd sleepily wandered in to make a pit stop. Or the time I inadvertently dropped liquid soap down her throat when we were playing at her bath. I am sure she still thinks I cleverly arranged for her cat Sugar to die in the Grim Garage Door, though I did not and the cat, who hated me, arranged for me to get the blame. And my gross, boy-remarks about bodily functions and running commentary on other drivers and people walking on the street will probably come back to haunt me, or her.

The worst part is when I see her acting like the shadow side of myself, using my snotty tone of voice and saying smart ass things I have said back to me, or having my prejudices about fat people, or the need for hard work, or constant money worries. No. The really worst part is when I see myself acting with her like my parents did with me, when the deeply serious sludge is stirred before my eyes and I am forced to decide whether to perpetuate the pattern, or change it. It is only through the pain of having "been there, done that" before that I force myself to go back and apologize, talk out arguments, negotiate what it would take to solve our problem, forgive and be forgiven.

I am glad, make that ecstatic, she is a girl. I would not have done well with the militaristic, macho toys, the violent, oppressive video games, or the ridiculous looking three-quarter length baggy shorts and wrinkled shirts - all of which are current cultural requirements for American boys.

Instead, I can offer other names for The Little Ponies (Oat-Breath, Pooter) or have interesting social discussions about the skinny, blonde, big boobed "perfect" Barbie, Ken, Scooter and Skipper. Every time the toy company came up with yet another "Fill-In-The-Blank Barbie" complete with required accoutrements, we'd come up with some ourselves. Thus, instead of Malibu Barbie, Swim Barbie, or Cheerleader Barbie, we decided there should be Barbies offering a broader range of appropriate roles for girls, big boobed or not. Doctor Barbie would go to work in white high heels, have a stethoscope, a bag, and a lab coat that turned into an evening dress when she went home to go out with Orderly Ken. Since our church has a woman priest we decided there should be a Priest Barbie, where (just as in real life) Mattel could make a zillion dollars from the required robes, stoles and other vestments and religious items she'd need. Instead of the gaudy pink plastic Barbie Dream House she would need the gaudy pink plastic Barbie All Faiths Chapel where she could eventually be ordained Bishop Barbie or maybe Archbishop of Can-ter-Barbie. Think of the things she'd need then! (A cope and mitre that turned into a hat and evening dress for when she went out with Cardinal Ken?) Our all time favorite, though, was our effort at cultural non-elitism: Garbage Barbie. She would dress in bib overalls, gloves, and a backwards gimme cap with Ken's Auto Parts on it, ride the back of a gaudy pink plastic garbage truck with recycle bins and have an array of sprayable odors depending on where she was working that day (Fish Market, Little Italy, Chinatown.)

The fact that we are sociologically and not biologically related is probably of great, and helpful, significance. We have never called each other step-anything and I have never, from the first day, thought of her as such. She has been my daughter since her mother and I married, and that's that. She calls me Dad and I call her Daud, among other things.

Not having any genetic progeny, I'm not sure about this, but it seems to me that I have somewhat less of a deep psychological investment in everything my daughter does than I would expect if she were otherwise. In that sense, she and I are freer to relate to each other than if we had invisible genetic chains enveloping each other. I am certain that that strains role issues when we are not sure whether to be parent/child, sibling, friend, or some combination. But it does make difficult behavior easier to tolerate.

In fact, it is clear to me that any time she acts out or does something inconsistent with my personal code of behavior or expectations for her social success, she is acting from her biological father's gene pool (which I refer to as "nut genes") for the consequences of which I am entirely unresponsible. My job, and I have taken it on with vigor, is to suppress the dysfunctional genetic baggage she has unfortunately acquired from the absent parent and introduce the incredibly healthy behaviors that have successfully arranged for me to survive to age forty-six, to accompany the wonderful traits acquired from her mother. Sort of like a gene transplant. Unfortunately this works both ways, as we have seen.

My daughter has just turned thirteen. If you felt a cold shudder run up your spine it is not because someone stepped on your grave, but because you empathize. From Ponies and Barbies we are now into groups with such enterprising names as Smashing Pumpkins, Meatloaf, and Ace of Base singing "All She Wants Is Another Baby" which is different from All She Wants Is Another Barbie.

I must hasten to add in her defense that she still maintains the same sweetness of character she had as a young child. More importantly, she is endowed with an unflagging sense of fairness (and ire at unfairness) that ultimately claims her attention even in the most heated child-parent conflicts. She is a good, even an easy teenager, if that is not an oxymoron.

Once again, just as before, her journey seems to be paralleling mine. She questions authority, tries out new clothes and ideas, (discarding each with equal alacrity based on their showing at the peer polls,) tests the limits and boundaries and so defines herself in relation to them, and deals with the exasperating, uncontrollable metamorphosis of her body exploding internally and externally, physically and emotionally, like popcorn in a microwave bag.

Likewise, I daily question my work and how much longer I want do to it. Does success stifle creativity? Would I be happier and better off quitting and writing full time? How would I provide for us? Where would I get healthcare? How could we keep this house? How do other people cash out at this age and go out on their own? Do they have families?

I try out new ideas and clothes, at least in my mind. I imagine different lifestyles, buy different clothing, more relaxed, less formal.

She wears only khaki shorts and jeans. I refuse to wear sportcoats and ties.

She casually announces that she'd really rather spend time with her friends instead of her parents, including on vacation. I plan trips for her mother and myself that allow for more free time and less sight-seeing.

She tells me that she likes my writing and wants to take samples to school. I find I enjoy some of her music and tell her so. Much to her surprise, I even borrow it.

I test the limits of the socially and religiously expected by writing what I think and believe, saying it out loud and in print just as she does with her writing for school, feeling finally confident to do so as she feels finally independent enough to try.

Where she deals with the daily surprises of bodily function and development, hair, breasts, periods, and zits, I deal with the similar astonishments of changed eyesight, greying hair, lazier libido, and precarious prostate.

She paints her toes red, a symbolic action that so changes my gestalt of her that it takes me days to recover. I grow a beard to her total chagrin. Eventually we remove both.

Perhaps I find myself on a parallel track with her because the forties are, in fact, a kind of adolescence. They are similar plateaus in our different lives. My daughter looks back on the freedom of childhood with a certain fondness and upon the independence and responsibility of young adulthood with some hesitation. I look back on the previous two decades of seemingly limitless possibility and ahead to the finite certainty of old age and death. It is as though we are dolphins swimming widely separated parallel courses in a huge ocean, having come up for air at the same time. Maybe that's why we talk together when we're not judging each other, compare notes when we are not defending our actions, share our stories to teach each other, and secretly hope to glean something which will ease our separate journeys.

I wonder if it will be the same later? How will we be when she is in her twenties and I am in my fifties; her thirties and my sixties, her forties (where I am now) and my seventies? Will we live long enough to find out?

I didn't sign up for a daughter. She was not in the picture I had painted to illustrate the novel of my life. But she has been an unexpected, undeserved, and sometimes unwanted gift who has been a surprising (and surprised) companion to growth, depth, meaning, and the discomforting reassurance that God indeed has a redeeming sense of humor. I only hope I have been the same to her.

My daughter's name is Michal Leah.

I love her.

GOD

God is having a midlife crisis.

Finally. It's about time.

God has had it entirely too easy.

All those years in the Old Testament, handing down commandments from on high, wrathing all over everybody, sending plagues when they were especially bad, getting the pick of the fatted calves, arguing with major and minor prophets, and winning, of course.

But there was a lot more negotiation back then than most preachers lead you to believe. Israel wanted a temple and a king, all for the right reasons, mind you, all to better serve God, they said. ("The better to serve you with, my dear.") And God fell for it, went along with the kids and ended up regretting it in the end, or in the meantime, actually, since God seems not to know much about ends, being constantly into new beginnings.

When all the rules were given, broken, renegotiated, broken again, fought over, renegotiated, exiled, returned, and Jesus had come, gone, and come back again, God's image had changed substantially. The mean old commandment giver with the angry voice of a really hacked off James Earl Jones after four double espressos had metamorphosed into Robert Young on herbal tea. Still the Creator though, God was now promising to "create a new heart in you." Maybe it was Marcus Welby.

The history of the Church over the last two thousand years has been a dialogue or a yelling match between those two voices, Jones and Young (sounds like a law firm, or a funeral home) in the form of schisms, wars, separations, theses, antitheses, social and political reforms, and a few good singable hymns like "Amazing Grace" and "The Saints of God."

Having done nearly all we could against each other, we turned on both of God's voices, didn't like either one because they were irrelevant and immaterial (as Perry Mason used to say) and declared the Deity Dead on the cover of Time Magazine in the Sixties. To those of us in our teens who had been dragged off to church every Sunday in little coats and ties or little dresses with patent leather shoes (which do *not* reflect up) it certainly looked that way.

For this was the decade of assassinations, Vietnam, free love, drugs, hippies, protests, nuclear threat, the War on Poverty, and the triumph of Richard Nixon, who a lot of people thought *was* God (Nixon included) partly because of his Secret Plan. If God had an adolescence, this was it. Everything seemed out of control. Emotions and hormones were everywhere dripping from the faucets of our minds (which was a popular folk tune of the time.) The universe was full of zits, like the crater filled face of the moon that man now walked over like a doormat.

It was a lot easier when there was Someone In Charge and therefore Someone To Blame. At least with James and Robert yelling at each other from different testaments, you felt like there was some structure, Someone Up There To Talk To or at least Scream At. But when the Sixties happened, Jim/Bob was silenced and adolescents were praying to just another out-of-control Adolescent. So it was true that the God I had known in the Fifties vanished like Houdini in the obscuring smoke of assassin guns, military bombs, police tear gas, and hippie joints.

As Liberation Theology swept the Third World, and Black Theology and the Theology of Hope careened across Worlds One and Two, it turned out that the rumors of God's death, like those of Mark Twain, were premature. The Church was another story.

Attendance plummeted in the seventies and eighties. We Boomers were busy getting accredited or finishing school or the service. We were getting jobs to support those expensive new families we never knew we'd have, along with the accompanying mortgages and the doctor bills and car payments.

I graduated from Union Theological Seminary in 1973. I had known I wanted to be an Episcopal priest since I was twelve, and the decision had little to do with God. I had a couple of excellent role models in our parish clergy and decided that the job of priesting combined all of what I seemed to like to do and was relatively good at: speech, drama, business, meeting people, leading meetings and writing. I would work out the fact that I was a Christian agnostic deep into Ayn Rand at a later date, such as seminary. I ultimately left Ayn Rand for Tom Robbins and maintain the same healthy, only much better informed, Christian agnosticism to this day.

Luckily, for God and myself, I have never had a parish. So far I have spent ten years in prison and fifteen in hospital chaplaincy. In both settings the focus is on people and problems without any thought to denomination or the kind of politics my friends in parishes have to endure. Also, free from church trappings and responsibilities, I think I have been able to watch more clearly God's progress from Sixties adolescence to Nineties Mid-Life Crisis.

Like the rest of us in our forties, things are happening in God's purview that nobody expected. The Berlin Wall is down, Russia is gone, Apartheid is dead and Mandela is President, Israel is making peace with everybody in the Mid-East, the U.S. is about to join the rest of the civilized world and adopt universal access to healthcare, CQI/TQM/Re-engineering processes are revolutionizing business and industry as trade barriers are falling worldwide, the Chunnel is open, and the Information Highway has no speed limit. Meanwhile the Church is still conducting services around Eighteenth Century milking schedules.

Now there is and always has been a major difference between God and the Church. From James Earl Jones through Robert Young and up to today the two have been generally out of synch. If this is God's Mid-Life Crisis, then the Church is still stuck in The Terrible Twos, intransigent about giving up what it has always known about itself and God, unwilling to get past the controlling joy of keeping God in a particular denominational jack-in-a-box building, theology, or creed.

But God in Mid-Life seems ready to shuck off both Jones and Young, whether the Church is ready for it or not. Theological images that made sense in an agrarian or even industrial world of political divisions are crumbling with the Berlin Wall. Rigid Biblical literalism has dissolved like the Soviet Union.

Instead of buying a sports car or having an affair, God metamorphosed from James Earl Jones and Robert Young into Whoopi Goldberg. Or maybe she's the Holy Spirit and God is The (androgynous) Force from Star Wars. And now The Force is changing into The Presence. See what Mid-Life Crisis does to you? You're changing all the time, with a different perspective than you had before.

God as The Presence makes more sense for the last decade of the Twentieth Century. If God is The Presence then our own human abilities can become linked with God's or not linked with God's as a matter of our choice, with consequences either way. Not consequences of Heaven or Hell but logical consequences in terms of being more or less who we are.

God as The Presence views the Bible as *metaphor*, not accurately transcribed inspired eye-witness videotaped film-at-eleven descriptions of actual events. Theologian James Sanders has said that "The Bible is not a model for morality, but a mirror for identity." We look into the Bible not to tell us what to do about the information explosion, instant communications, customer service, welfare reform or the homeless. We look to the Bible to see who we *are* in relationship to God, metaphorically translating the stories and seeking process instead of direction, interaction rather than accomplishment. We invite and trust that The Presence is with us and will continue to be wherever our respective journeys may lead.

This makes things much shakier for us all, God included, because the roles are blending into each other like whipped cream in jello. It was a lot easier to have Someone To Blame, along with the same Someone To Ask. Because the purpose of prayer changes here too. The purpose of prayer becomes *presence* not outcome. Prayer, whatever it is, whether booting the system or actually communicating with it or keeping lines open, becomes inviting The Presence from our end, opening to It as Skywalker did with The Force and thereby was most empowered to be fully himself.

The Atonement theory then goes the way of Apartheid, metamorphosing from rigidly held belief that made sense to people in a particular time period into a broader, changed metaphor that addresses what we have come to learn about God and ourselves now. Not only is there "neither Greek nor Jew, male nor female," but there is neither Christian nor Buddhist, Moslem or Taoist. Many paths, same mountain.

Jesus then becomes someone who didn't know it all ahead of time, who struggled with his identity as we all do, gradually realizing that events were unfolding in a manner that would inevitably lead to his death at the hands of a nervous government, not an unheard of scenario even today. Resurrection, as much a surprise to Jesus as to the Disciples, becomes the best word they had at the time to describe the incredible thing that had happened to him and them together. Whatever it was, the event of experiencing Jesus repeatedly after his death galvanized a rag-tag powerless group of rapidly defecting individuals into a fully committed, mutually supportive body who were willing to risk martyrdom to share what they knew to be true.

May The Presence be with you. And also with you.

The death/resurrection experience is something we continually have over and over again in our lives. Being reminded of it through the metaphors of the Bible brings us hope as we read of forgiveness, mercy, and renewal for ourselves and others, based on the ethic of compassion.

Now this theology has tremendous implications for the Church. The words of liturgy will change further toward the use of inclusive language and imagery and away from Atonement. The polity and corporate structure of religious organizations will change toward inclusive decision making as the boundaries between clergy and laity fade like the borders in NAFTA.

Already some congregations are asking the same questions corporate management has begun to ask. Why do we do what we do? Why do we do it this way? Why do we have services on Sunday morning, of all times? Given the need for leisure and the demands on the family that already tax their time together, why not do church on Thursday night and not have to get up the one day you and your kids may have together to sleep in, go to the movies, or read the paper? Why not have church in the round? Why not have e-mail instead of bulletins? Why not have weekly neighborhood house church services organized by geographical areas and "big church" services once a month, or quarterly?

The incredible popularity of current cultural religious material is no accident. The focus on angels (if only Rubens knew he'd be a billionaire today,) on books about spiritual direction, the interest in death/ dying and near-death experiences, and the Hollywood movies dealing with afterlife, indicate a clear and urgent hunger for spiritual feeding that has found the Church's cupboard largely bare and meaningless. Thus the seeming schizophrenic developments of New Age religions on the one hand (the left one of course) and the increasing growth of the Religious Right on the other (right?) Both evidence the current desire for certainty in a world full of change.

But the New Agers lose their appeal to me in their discounting of the Dark Side, their refusal to acknowledge the ability in each of us to destroy, manipulate, and lie for our own personal gain. At the penitentiary I learned that any one of us is capable of committing any crime, no matter how despicable. There is no such thing as purity of spirit in that sense, unless it acknowledges both of what the Eastern religions call Yin and Yang within us. Anyone who has survived to forty-six knows this up close and personal.

And the Religious Right, popular though they are with their attractively simple solutions, pat answers and self-righteous judgementalism, simply don't know how to read the Bible. They read it selectively, focusing almost exclusively on the Dark Side and their solution for keeping it in check (which often involves a check.) If the New Agers are Robert Young gone awry, the Religious Right are James Earl Jones on speed.

I claim no expert or special knowledge as to how this will all turn out. Sometimes it seems that God's Mid-Life Crisis is halfway between old age and youth, that God started out old like a Vulcan and ages backwards. (Is that why the Old Testament precedes the New Testament?) In that case, God is a lot younger than before and on the way toward new infancy. Funny how that parallels my own growth. I knew much more with unchallengeable certainty when I was nineteen.

Only a God struggling with the forties could be open to this kind of introspection and change, could be willing to develop together a different relationship now that the old structures are crumbling and no longer meaningful or useful. Because that is exactly what our forties are about.

The appropriate metaphor for all these struggles is the story of Jacob wrestling with the angel. We wrestle with God as we recreate new images of each other and develop new relationships. The Church wrestles with God as its structures crumble like the Berlin Wall. God wrestles with God to re-emerge (resurrect) all three in some ongoing way.

Jacob refuses to let the angel go until the angel "blesses" him - gives him a name. The name that we get may not be the one we want. In fact, if the Bible stories are to be believed, it will not be the one we want, one that comforts and confirms where and who we already are. Instead it will be one that challenges us, demands action from us, creates new images within us and gives us clearer understanding of ourselves and our community. As it wrestles, the Church will also get a new name.

And so will God.

But our names are not received without the pain of struggle, the physical, emotional wrestling and the suffering of injuries to our certitude. The equivalent of Jacob's thigh being put out of joint by the angel may be evidence of the strength with which we cling to what we think we know - about religion and about ourselves as we go through our forties - so that we come out at the other end marked for the rest of our lives by that struggle and reminded of it with the occasional limp or the ability to forecast the weather by the ache in our hip.

So I do my fatherly duty and drag my daughter off to church nearly every Sunday. I don't care what she wears as long as she goes with me. I usually wear jeans or a running suit, much to the suppressed ire (or envy) of the conservative eight o'clockers. I tell myself I want her to go so she can be familiar with the stories and images of Scripture that figure so powerfully in Western culture; so she will be culturally literate, able to understand and appreciate Shakespeare and t.s. elliot. And I want her to experience the healing rhythm of the reconciling liturgy that hopefully will be metaphorically interpreted for her either by me now or by someone else in the future when she really needs it - when she is twenty and thirty and forty.

But the truth is I don't want to go alone. I like her presence, as it is further evidence of The Presence my daughter and I invite into each other's lives in our uncertain, changing times; she as she wanders bonking her head on the obstacles of adolescence, me as I do the same through my forties. I like holding hands as we enter the church together (if no one she knows is watching) and leave together separately holding hands with God.

Like they say in the stock market: "Past performance is no guarantee of future developments." But the spiritual metaphors are clearly stacked in the direction that we will all survive our transitions and meet again in the Great By And By of our fifties and beyond. I can't wait to see who God is then.

U-TROU

"Dad..." My ten-year-old daughter held my hand as we walked down the street. "...Today I learned in science class..." (this was a euphemism for *SEX EDUCATION* and I cringed, not knowing what topic it would be *this* time) "...that boys should wear boxers because it doesn't hold their testicles up so close to their body." She looked at me, concerned. "Maybe you should switch?"

When I recovered my breath from cardiac arrest, I vowed to relieve her of laundry folding duty. But I got to thinking. What if she was right? What if fortysomething years of wearing "briefs" was slowly causing me day by day to develop some insidious terminal illness caused by overheated testicles, like a car that slowly drips coolant from the radiator until one day, suddenly, without warning, at seventy miles an hour, the whole engine melts into a solid block and the car hurtles out of control off a bridge?

In my job at the hospital I have learned that such things are possible, so I considered the issue carefully, paranoically, because every day I see new variations of devastation wreaked on totally

45

unsuspecting people. I also considered the issue skeptically because I did not actually want to give up my "briefs."

Why do men call them "briefs" anyway? Is it because "underpants" sounds too personal - or too feminine? Actually, the only people I ever heard call them "briefs" are the absolutely perfect mannequin models that none of us look like in the ads. The always precise Germans call them Leibwasche - "abdomen-linen." In more poetic France they are "lingerie." In my grossly utilitarian college dorm in 1965 they were called *"u-trou"* (under-*trou*sers) and I still call them that. "U-trou" is short and descriptive. You don't mince words and you get the picture.

If you are a woman on a first date and want to get a telling portrait of the man, don't ask him his sign or how much money he makes or how many toys he has. Ask him to give you a history of his underwear. It will tell you everything.

I know I started out with diapers because my older brother constantly reminds me at embarrassing moments how awful it was when he changed them. They were cloth and soft and gave direct, honest feedback, letting you know when you had filled them or exploded out the sides. They were not the modern artificial, toss into the garbage can and gross out everyone for miles kind with computer intelligence built into the crotch lying about whether the kid is deluged or slimy.

These old fashioned cloth diapers, I am told, were snug, which may be the first clue as to which vitally important decision the man makes in later life: briefs or boxers. If your Democrat mother tied you into the diaper so tight your eyes popped out you choose briefs. If she was a Republican laissez faire trickle down mother, you choose boxers.

My generation grew up with briefs. We were the Boomers, from neat post-war houses with tidy yards and bedrooms, oilcloth on our elementary school tables, hair and nails clean for church on Sunday, in midget suits with briefs underneath. The only time we saw boxers was on old men like our fathers.

When I was six, I wore briefs with various boy-things on them: airplanes, guns, horses, cactus (ouch), cowboy hats and Howdy Doody. This was in pre-historic times when girls had nothing to do with such images. By the time I got to junior high everyone wore just plain white Hanes or Jockey briefs.

I seem to recall some accelerated maturational or "cool" status attributed to one brand. Whichever it was I wore the other one. I am certain this is the reason for my current emotional scarring, causing me to write such things as this. There are other exact psychological-type correlations (similar to the Myers-Briggs) for men who grew up wearing u-trou with labels in the back from Sears, Montgomery-Ward, K-Mart, and Penny's. There are u-trou trauma support groups to address these different types and their corresponding co-dependencies, phobias, and emotional disorders.

High school in the 'sixties lent itself to briefs. They provided us with a way down deep secure feeling in an otherwise insecure world of nuclear threat. The sexual revolution was just beginning and, contrary to the lies we all told, it made us just as nervous as Vietnam, drugs, assassinations, the War on Poverty, and Barry Goldwater.

Briefs were tight, reflecting a popular song: "Everything is all right, up tight, out of sight." They rode up like a truss under even tighter jeans to keep second period Math class erections in place and caught the pee that didn't shake off at the urinal. ("No matter how you jump and dance, the last few drops go in your pants.") They also showed the goods better if you ever got that far, and they didn't look stupid when you took them off and put them with the other dirty laundry under your bed.

By the time I got to college, briefs were available in "low rise," "bikini," and in assorted colors. The guys in my dorm paraded through the hall and in and out of each other's rooms displaying the latest options amid gross comments and rude suggestions. ("You drop the potato down the *front*, you idiot!") I think we wore colors for much the same reason as male peacocks and mallards - we liked to show them off.

Low risers and bikinis stayed in style for the next decade or so. They looked good as long as our twenties and thirties physiques fit neatly into them. With the advent of Ronald Reagan, boxers made a comeback. There is a direct political correlation here.

I never understood boxers. I guess the name had a more masculine sound to it until you pictured those hunched-over guys in their baggy EVERLAST shorts slugging each other's brains out in a small ring filled with smoke, one light bulb, and a short, bald guy in a striped shirt. The image tarnished even more when you added blood and bruises and cauliflower ears. Why would anyone want to emulate that?

And why did girls start wearing them? They wore them over their own bikini panties (why is it panties for girls?) or under regular shorts so they stuck out about knee length. Then guys started doing the same, showing the edge of their boxers under their shorts. Too gross for me, this fashion fad further forced me to cling, perhaps in political retaliation, to the time honored u-trou style of my childhood - the "brief" - even though I could not find any with airplanes.

Then I turned forty-five, and something happened to my body. Let me preface this by saying I am a runner. Not a jogger, a runner. I run 4 miles three times a week and do longer runs of 6-10 miles on weekends. I have completed two marathons and many half marathons. I wear running shorts of various shortness, and do not consider myself overweight or flabby. But I recently noticed that the low rise briefs in my u-trou drawer were rising a lot lower than they used to.

My first thought, of course, was that a certain appendage was enlarging, which either meant great good fortune or terminal illness. I desperately hoped for the former. But the low risers and the few remaining bikinis of my younger days began to look silly after repeated washings, fadings and shrinkings. They looked even worse when I put them on. I found myself frequently getting "crotchies" (the male equivalent of "wedgies") at work. When I reached in my pocket to inconspicuously pull them down, the waistband gave me rug burn.

I am basically a utilitarian person. If it works, do it. If it doesn't work and you can't make it work, forget it and go on to the thing that does work. I put the low risers in the back of the drawer (thinking surely this was a temporary occurrence) and wore only regular brief u-trou.

Then one day my sweet, wonderful younger-than-I spouse emptied my u-trou drawer of all but one pair of *boxers* which she had secretly purchased for me, partly as a joke, partly as an unsubtle recommendation. It was a morning when she knew I would dress mainly in the dark and half asleep and when I had a particularly stressful presentation at work. Her note said simply: "Hang loose."

I did, or rather I tried to. I knew as I put them on I would hate them. Through heavy lidded eyes I stared in the mirror at the striped boxers I had just donned. Unlike the firm fitting, diaper-memory-like secure u-trou I had always worn, these looked baggy. They looked big. They looked old. They looked like my father's as I remember him standing in the bathroom slapping on Old Spice in his ancient sleeveless tank t-shirt with holes in it and his skinny blue-veined bird-legs sticking out the bottoms of the baggy boxers. My runner's legs were firmer than his, but the look was similar. Too similar.

I was right. I did hate them. And I would find a way to wreak appropriate revenge on my wife. Soon. Perhaps I would steal a pair of *her* u-trou to wear to work and purposely have a car wreck on the way so she would have to come to the emergency room to claim me and be totally mortified.

But as I walked into the closet a strange sensation occurred. I realized that, instead of the normal tightly bound compression of the Crown Jewels with a force that turns coal to diamonds, I felt as though they were freely suspended in mid air, as if hanging over the edge of a building, dangling precariously in the wind, almost as though they *weren't there* because I couldn't feel them.

This was new territory. Could it be that we wear briefs to hold the Crown Jewels close to the body as a reminder that they are *there*? So we don't *forget*? What would it be like to dangle for a day? To follow my wife's admonition to "hang loose?" Would I remember where they were? What they were for?

Trust that - untrussed - they would not fall off?

I reached for my trousers and pulled them on over the boxers. It was a bizarre feeling, like going skinny dipping for the first time when you can't quite believe you're actually doing it.

I smiled. So *this* was what it was like. Maybe I would smile the whole day being the only one knowing I was walking down the hall dangling the Jewels in the breeze.

I did, and it was great. No more the constant "crotchies" and the surreptitious internal wrenching down of briefs at awkward moments. Oh sure, there were the few times I wondered if, after the urinal, the last few drops bypassed the boxers and plummeted downward to my trousers or socks. That never happened, a nd mostly they were more comfortable than the other, safe, secure u-trou I had worn all my life.

Comfort! That was an interesting criterion for choosing u-trou! What a change! What a paradigm shift! Full of enthusiasm, I decided that day to switch to boxers. I anxiously awaited the next men's sale at the large department store in the mall and raced to stock up on my new find.

Once there, my courage failed me.

At first I walked by the old brief rack and proceeded to the boxers. I leafed through the hermetically sealed packages of individually wrapped u-trou and picked out six pairs I liked. They were your fairly standard plaids, stripes, and checks. I hate paisley. It looks like you have disease-crazed amoebas circling your butt. Worse, it looks like someone is observing you under a microscope, comparing the size of your genitals to paramecia.

I headed to the check-out counter but was stopped in my tracks by a sudden sense of wrong-doing. The preponderance of nostalgic u-trou history arose in my brain to question this radical change. What if this was a fluke? What if it didn't work out? What if, in the middle of a conversation I suddenly had a panic attack of unsupported dangling and totally lost my identity and self confidence? Could I really stand up in front of an audience and give a presentation in boxers? Would I be too loose? Not enough structural support? Perhaps it was my German heritage. Germans wear briefs made of carbon steel. The even more precise German word is the same descriptive one they use for brassiere: "Holdzumupundschtopzumpfloppin."

I turned around, put three of the boxers back on the rack and picked up a three-pack of the good old reliable, uncomfortable briefs. This way I compromised with my angst. I could transition my way into boxers, wear the appropriate u-trou depending on my mood and my work responsibilities.

I put my six pairs of u-trou on the counter and the woman (why is it always a *woman* in the men's under-wear department - they wouldn't put a *man* in the brassiere department) tried not to smirk as she rang them up. She knew from experience that men my age were universally making this transition, beating drums and sitting in sweat lodges together as they work through the emotional trauma of dropping their briefs for boxers, often with primal screams.

Her back was turned as I glanced at the display on the counter. It was the next generation of u-trou for the very young and very stupid. It was a *thong*, otherwise defined as front cup with a string up your butt. Perhaps it is my age or my lack of imagination, but why would anyone pay money (especially *that much* money) for a guaranteed permanent wedgie?

She turned around, knowing I had been looking at them.

"It's not for you," she said sardonically. "Only the college guys buy them." She stuffed my purchases in a bag. "It puts a thong in their heart," she said flatly.

And butt-floss in their hiney.

I nodded and walked off only semi-victoriously. I had begun yet another life transition, probably too cautiously as I am wont to do. I would test out the boxer u-trou in various settings, or sittings: doing a lecture, under jeans, under shorts in summer (hard to imagine, but possible), driving long distances, on an airplane. There was so much to explore.

As I got in the car something happened. I had known all along I was deeply bothered about this change. I first had thought it was simply the giving up of the old familiar u-trou which had carried me, literally, through my youth and young adulthood; a kind of nostalgic reluctance to part with favorite fond memories of u-trou past, like a kid giving up a blankie. But when I tossed the package onto the passenger seat, the briefs fell out with a pair of boxers on top of them.

The transition was visibly clear. The linear progression disturbed me. The move from briefs to boxers was a sign of aging, a move from youth into what we joking call "middle age" with all its attendant losses of hair, vision and prowess. But the terror was not in the loss of my briefs and the movement to boxers; that change actually held promise for me. The terror was in the logical projection to the next step — the loss of my boxers in exchange for adult diapers in a nursing home when the cycle rejoins itself at the end. Given our Boomer demandingness and the genetic American propensity to make a buck, our adult diapers in 2012 will have Howdy Doodys and Barbies on them, probably together, possibly coupled. But it still did not make the prospect desireable.

In a primordial rage against the darkness of the hopefully far future night, I went back to the store, made another purchase and drove home. The next day, when I was at work in my boxers giving a lecture on death to a class of nursing students, my wife opened her own u-trou drawer to find a tiny red object with a note. She held the thing suspended by its string and read the altered words of Jim Croce:

Every time I tried to tell you,
The words just came out wrong.
So I guess I'll say 'I love you'
With a thong.

SHAVING

"Daaaaddd!" The familiar voice of the ten year old daughter-in-distress rang from behind the shower door.

"Whaaaat?" came my reply from my desk where I was happily employed at my computer, indicating that this had better be important, something in the "blood or bones showing" category.

"I need help with my pits."

"Great," I muttered under my breath. I saved the latest piece of great literature on the screen and extricated myself from the comfort of my well worn leather chair, desperately wishing mother could instantly return from out of town to resume her duties as primary overseer of the newly acquired skills of shaving legs and pits.

The first time at this was a fiasco. Her mother and I spent the better part of an evening going over with her the fine art of Western culture for girls coming of age - applying a white foamy substance and a sharpened steel blade to her still baby soft skin to shave the perfectly natural leg and underarm hair that women in every other culture on earth seem to find fashionable to leave totally alone.

I am a recent Dad. This child came as a part of the marriage package, but without instructions. I had never intended to *have* children, much less a girl child of ten who was rapidly advancing into puberty at what seemed to be warp speed.

Her little girlfriends started developing equally little chest bumps at age nine, due, I am told by a reliable pediatrician, to a "better" diet than we had as kids. (You mean Twinkies and Root Beer *suppress* chest bumps?) This same pediatrician tells me that girls either develop hair first or breasts first. Unfortunately for my daughter, her body won hair in this physical lottery, much to her dismay. Her mother and I assured her that her protruding little baby belly, about which she constantly worried, would eventually move in and up to provide wonderfully adequate breasts very soon. We hoped.

So on this second shaving outing I was called to the bath to do battle with unreachable (by her) underarm hair.

"Why are you squinting?" she asked.

"I do that when I'm concentrating," I said, trying to *see* the damned things.

"Not so *fast*!" she squealed as I zipped the tiny razor under her upraised arm. "You'll cut me!"

"No, I won't. Trust me, I've done this for years," I replied, wondering how in the world I ever ended up in this situation. "There, that's one down. Think you can get the other one?"

"I'll try," she said, sounding relieved that I had not totally severed her right armpit. There is often method to a father's seeming madness.

"Oh, you're doing great!" I said, as she slowly dragged the razor up and over the stubbly black hairs.

"I can't do any more," she cried. "I'll nick it and it'll hurt."

She handed me the razor.

"Okay. But next time it's all yours, right?"

"Thank you, Daddy," she said, in that sweet, sing-songy way that makes me do absolutely anything at all that she could ever ask. I was not told about this in the prenuptial agreement.

It was actually a sweet moment between her and I, one of the last few times that we both would be unembarrassed as her body metamorphosed into the privacy of adolescence. And I was pleased that she trusted me enough to let me be a part of her growing up.

It had not been that way for me at that tender age, and I told her so. She still enjoys hearing stories of when her mother and I were her age. She even *asks* to hear such stories that begin with the soon-to-be-hated words "When *I* was your age..." That is because she hasn't started dating yet, at which point my wife and I will develop terminal stupidity.

As she sat on the carpet in her (my) extra large t-shirt with a towel turbined around her head, I recalled my own first experience with shaving. My best friend, Monty, and I turned 13 about the same time. Not having the modern benefit of "better diets" we were physically retarded in the facial hair category. In today's politically correct environment we would be called "beard challenged." Because we believed the blonde fuzz on our soft faces to be the precursor of Norselike carpets of hair, we agreed to buy each other razors for our birthdays, thereby saving ourselves the incredible embarrassment of having to buy them for ourselves and bring them home to the certain ridicule of our respective families.

"So, you think you *need* that?" my Germanic father who never bought anything he didn't *need* asked when Monty presented me with the Gillette Safety Razor and two packs of Blue Blades.

"Yeah. Sure he does, Mr. Meyer," Monty piped up, knowing I would mouth the same rehearsed lines at his house sometime the next weekend. "I've been noticing it for some time now, and that's why I got it for him."

What are friends for, anyway, if not to offer supporting lies in moments of embarrassment, to be remembered for a lifetime?

"And did you ever cut yourself, when you first started?" my daughter asked, flicking water on me now from brushing her wet hair.

"Well," I grinned, "...about a week later I had to go to a drugstore to buy a styptic pencil."

"A what?"

"It's a little pencil-looking thing made of

unknown, probably toxic waste chemicals that, when applied to the skin, immediately stops the bleeding and starts you screaming."

"I don't want one."

"No, you don't."

"What happened?"

"I had had a bad experience the night before. You have to understand that in 1960 the term 'safety razor' was an oxymoron. I always got the setting wrong so that either I shaved off the foam, leaving the hairs untouched, or I took off skin down to the jawbone."

"Daaaaaad!"

"Sorry. Like you, I was afraid of cutting myself - and so I did, everywhere. I looked like tiny little juvenile delinquents had taken tiny knives to my face. I had nicks and little bloody lines the length of the razor blade everywhere from the tops of my sideburns to the sides of my Adam's apple.

"Monty was in front of me in the drugstore check out line and there were some elderly women behind me. I should have bought a bunch of things and slipped the pencil in with it. But no, I only had enough money to buy the one item. This was in prehistoric times before they had scanners and talking cash registers and the clerk actually had to do something difficult, like read the price."

"Daddy..."

"Anyway, I tossed the styptic pencil onto the counter and the cashier - who was only a little older than I was - took one look at it and one look at my sliced up face and started laughing out loud. Then, of course, Monty saw the connection and he laughed with her and then the old ladies behind me started chuckling."

My unsympathetic daughter was now doubled over in laughter herself.

"I still carry the scars, so to speak.."

"What else? When you were a teen-ager, I mean."

"Funny you should ask. I just remembered shaving my grandfather."

"Does this mean I can stay up late?"

"It's not *that* long a story."

"Darn. How old was he?" she asked, fascinated with age and family history, and a new way to avoid bedtime.

"He was in his eighty's then. Every Sunday my Dad - your Grandpa - and I would go to early church and then go down to Mom and Pop's to get them ready to come to our house for the day. Part of the routine was for my Dad to shave Pop with an electric razor. One Sunday I asked if I could do it, this honor of running a buzzing machine over Pop's face. It had to do with manhood, somehow."

"Spare me the lecture on puberty, please, Daddy."

"Right. When we got there, Pop was in his sturdy black rocking chair, his red checkered flannel shirt buttoned up around his neck as it was year round. He was the epitome of old German stock. He looked like one of those bulldogs with beer steins you've seen in the pictures in Grandpa's basement. He sat there, immobile, as I approached his face with the electric razor.

"I had never felt the old man's face before. It was tougher than I thought. Though he never opened his tight-lipped mouth, I could smell the cigar smoke on his breath. I held his sagging skin taut as his tough old whiskers poked like tiny staples into my sensitive fingers. I did the best I could - remember, like the cash register, this was in the Middle Ages of electronics, somewhere between the transistor radio and color t.v. - and the razor wasn't all that great. My Dad had to finish up for me as I sat mesmerized by son caring for father, Dad squinting his eyes just as I squinted mine shaving you.

"I'll never forget the toughness of Pop's skin and the spineyness of the whiskers and the way he sat Sphinx-like with his gnarled fingers intertwined and his eyes closed until I finished. He never said 'Thank you.'"

"That was rude..."

"No, not for Germans. He did mutter 'Bitte shoen'."

"Meaning?"

"Sort of meaning 'Okay.' I remember wondering at the time if my beard would ever be as prickly as his, or my skin as saggy and tough."

My daughter reached up and touched my face. "Not yet. But you're getting there."

"Thanks."

She sat back down. "What happened in college?"

"What makes you think anything happened in college?"

"Daddy, my friend's big sister says *everything* happens in college."

"You just want to stay up late."

"Yeah," she grinned, "...but I also want to know."

I decided to indulge her. "It was my sophomore year. You'll learn that your sophomore year in college is a big time of change, sort of like right now. You need to try things, test your wings, experiment, and it's your last chance until you retire at sixty-five and nobody cares anymore so you can do what you want. So I grew a beard."

"DADDY!" She looked at me incredulously.

"Yep. And I must say it looked great. I grew it for the reason John Steinbeck grew his."

"Because it made him a great writer like you?" She batted her eyes.

"I love it when you get your lines right. But no, that wasn't the reason at the time. Steinbeck said he grew his beard for the same reason the peacock shows off his feathers, because it looks good. Unfortunately I was the *only* person who thought it looked good. The old ladies in the college cafeteria where I worked breakfast every morning thought I looked like the *Devil* - literally. One of them swore she was going to hold me down and shave it off."

"What *did* you look like?"

"I looked like *Hell*, literally."

"Daaaaaad!"

"Well, I did. I looked really sinister, my face kind of drawn and gaunt, pulling my eyes closer together and shrinking my jaw into a narrow 'V' of red and black hairs."

She grabbed my chin with her still wet from the bath hand and dragged my face into the light from the lamp.

"You *do* have red hairs in there! Where did they come from?"

"That's what *I* wanted to know. I thought it gave credence to the theory that I was adopted or of different fathering."

"But how could that...?"

"Another story...It turned out I called my brother and asked him where the *red* came from."

Having finished face inspection, she returned my chin to my chair.

"And...?"

"And he told me he wondered the same thing the first time *he* grew a beard. So he asked Grandma and she said that when she was a little girl she had red hair!"

"Grandma had *red* hair?!"

"Yep! Already I was learning about my family through this wonderful experience....but there was much more to learn, as I was to find out when I got home from college for Christmas break."

"What happened?"

"Your Grandpa wouldn't let me in the house."

With the towel on her head and the Cheshire cat smile on her face, I could tell this little girl was liking this story much too much, and that she would remind me of this scenario at the appropriate time, say, when she has her nose pierced.

"I came to the back door and he looked out the window and turned around and wouldn't let me in. Thought I was a Commie pinko radical."

"What's that?"

"Not a Republican. So your Grandma came to the door and unlocked it and expressed her dismay, disbelief and disappointment, all of which quite obviously confirmed that growing it was the right decision. But then they played dirty pool with me."

"They cut it off in your sleep?"

"Worse. They sicked my girlfriend on me. They called her to come over and tell me to shave it off."

"And you did?"

"I confess, I weakened when she said she'd have trouble kissing me through the stubble on my lips. It was another Samson number. I shaved my beard that night. I remember looking in the mirror, watching my smooth cheeks reappear after months of slow, careful, day by day covering, and I remember telling myself not to worry, that I could always do this again someday. In the meantime, I would daily scrape the little hairs down to the skin to appease the societal pressures that you, tonight, are appeasing in the same way."

My daughter's heavy eyelids slowly closed and

opened.

"Bedtime," I said.

"Right," she yawned, forcing herself out of the chair and letting me guide her to her room.

"Actually, I have always had this theory that shaving causes cancer."

"Daaaaaad!"

"No, really!" I said tucking her into her soft bed, surrounded by bunnies and other stuffed critters. "I think that scraping your skin and letting in the artificial substances in the soap allows the body to soak up cancer-causing chemicals and that's the reason more civilized places in the world don't mess with all this stuff."

"So...I *shouldn't* shave my legs and pits?"

"Naw, go on ahead and do it. Until we make enough money to move to Europe where civilized people know that shaving is ridiculous, unnecessary, and socially acceptable. Until then, you still have to go to sixth grade tomorrow where the other girls will be smooth, sleek and hair free."

"Night, Dad. I love you," she said in her sleepiest, and to me, her sweetest voice.

"I love you too, sweetie-pie, hair or no hair."

"Me too you, Daddy. You know what?"

"What?"

"Shaving is fun if you don't cut yourself."

"Yeah," I replied, pulling the covers up to her neck. "Just like life."

And she drifted off to hairless sleep, where

shaving made no difference at all in her social status, her place on the sixth grade food chain of importance, or her place in my heart.

SANDWICH

I remember the first time my mother wasn't there.

I was driving her to the hospital to see my dad, who had had a heart attack, and I asked her a simple question about where she wanted to eat. She just stared out the window. It wasn't that she didn't *want* to answer. But the complex neurological pathways in her brain had somewhere gone awry. She *couldn't* answer.

In recent years, my father had become the strong caretaker for her. As her health declined and she had trouble walking or doing things around the house, he had picked up the slack. Now, for the first time in his eighty five years, he was flat on his back in ICU. She was home without him, and the thought that someday soon this situation might be permanent had stunned and overwhelmed her, terrified her into passive silence. The doctor later called it a TIA, a small stroke or series of small strokes.

It was as if, in that long moment in which she could not answer, my past and her future came to an end.

The mother was gone:

- who had laid on my bedroom floor and colored with me, who could shade with Crayolas and keep them in the lines.

- who had whacked my older brother on the shoulder with the yardstick and then nearly wet her pants laughing with us when the yardstick broke.

- who consistently forgot the rolls in the oven at every huge Sunday dinner.

- who was generous to a fault and the emotional mainstay of the three males in the house.

- who was always able to think clearly about an issue and look at both sides before deciding.

Up until that moment, I must have expected that my mother would always be there with the same abilities and humor; in short, that she would always be herself. But now she wasn't. Those past images no longer played like a movie that continued into the present; they were suddenly frozen, still frame photographs to look back on and remember how we used to be.

For her the future became threateningly clear. The fragile stability with which my aging parents managed to conduct their daily lives had shattered. What had happened to most of their friends was happening to them.

Somewhere in the deep recesses of her mind, she knew that one of them would have an "event" - as the doctors called it - a broken hip was the most usual, but it could also be a heart attack, a stroke, a cold that worsened into pneumonia, something that would crack the thin veneer of normalcy holding them together. Once broken, it could be patched, but not repaired. The crack would continue to enlarge, splitting them, eventually, from each other.

In the long moment of our encounter, my mother and I saw these things clearly for the first time. And in that moment our relationship changed. Our roles reversed.

I spoke for her and made the decision. She acquiesced.

In the days and years that followed, she would flicker like the flame of a candle. At times she would burn brightly and be entirely herself, talkative, funny, sarcastic. At other times the flame would sputter into tiredness and silence.

Dad was another story.

We found him sitting up in ICU drinking coffee and winking at the nurses, who of course thought him charming. ICU nurses love feisty old men who actively try to sneak out of their unit, even if it is for a smoke.

He was, as usual, full of bullshit and bravado, ready to go home, threatening to sign himself out, to leave AMA - against medical advice - rising to the occasion for my obviously worried mother; small setback, nothing to worry about really, back in the saddle in no time.

As it turned out, he was right. It was a small setback and he came home from the hospital the next day. But the frail balance of interdependence that they had developed to hide the truth of increasing infirmity had been upset. And even he had to notice.

My father had always been loud and boisterous, dominating conversations with endless stories, unable to sit for five minutes without jumping up to do something, smoke a cigarette or refill the coffee. Now he sat longer, and, although he still expressed strong opinions, he was willing to be overruled by his two sons, or at least led by our suggestions.

As I sat with them at the kitchen table, the traditional gathering place around which all important family decisions had been made or announced, I realized that I was part of The Sandwich Generation - I had responsibilities not only for managing my daughter and her upbringing, but now for managing my parents in their slow decline.

How could they do this to me? I was supposed to be the son and they the parents. They were supposed to know what to do for themselves without my input. They were supposed to remain the strong couple, incredibly active in the community, doing volunteer work at the State Hospital, attending weekly dinners and club meetings, going out to shows and social events, having people over Saturday night to play cards till the wee hours and still managing to get up and go to the eight o'clock service every Sunday. I was supposed to remain the distant son, checking in weekly as we led separate but connected lives. A well defined role for everyone, everyone in their role.

Now that fantasy was over, forever shattered with other myths we confront in our forties, like immortality, and perfect health, eyesight, hair, shapes, and children.

How do we make this transition, this quantum leap from child to parent? It happened instantly, with no one noticing, no time to adjust, to get our bearings, to know what to do and how to act. We were all making it up as we went along, and it was awkward and uncomfortable and strange. There was a sense in which we all resented it, being knocked unwittingly out of our familiar, if not comfortable, relationships, like stars suddenly falling from a well known constellation. There was imbalance and anger, embarrassment and rage from them at the undeniable acknowledgement of their aging and loss of ability; resentment on my part for having to switch roles and take care of those who had always been the caretakers; grief all around at the loss of who we were.

How do we become what we have defined ourselves in relation to all our lives? Having always been the rebellious, independent kid defying their expectations, then exceeding them in my own way, I was now being called upon to help them maintain the lifestyle against which I had rebelled.

Though I had, like most children, adopted most of the values I had learned from my mother and father; trust, fairness, commitment to the community and to share with those less fortunate - there were significant differences in the way those values were interpreted in my life. We simply saw the world differently, with different prejudices, different desires, different insights. Given these significant differences, how would it ever be possible for me to parent my parents?

And it could not come at a more difficult time. As my own daughter moved into adolescence, she was actively defining herself against my values and beliefs.

It was as though my head was spinning, Exorcist-like, in both directions, trying like crazy to watch both situations at once, and react to them with some sense of consistency and logic while my feelings were out of control.

The upper piece of sandwich bread pressed down on me in the form of demands and expectations for caregiving that could not ever be met from the long distance between where they lived in Ohio and my home in Texas. Hints about physical problems and suggestions about visits raised old deep guilt from childhood failures and disappointments. Watching them stubbornly fight every step of the way, refusing to give ground to disability or disease and maintaining the facade of normalcy at all costs, raised the spectre of my own aging and how I would handle it, the fear of becoming what I was vividly witnessing.

Would I be doing this when I reached their age? What was I doing now in my forties to set the stage for my aging? I was doing things they had never done. I ran three times a week, watched my diet, limited caffeine, sugar and fat intake. Unlike my father who had smoked since he was fourteen, I never picked up the habit. Like him, and like my entire German family, I enjoyed beer, though recently I had switched to the non-alcoholic brands. Also like both my father and mother, I was an industrious workaholic who thought anything less than a sixty hour work week was slacking.

The lower, daughter piece of bread pressed upward with equal force. As she struggled with her own growth I felt pushed to warn her of the mistakes of her grandparents as I interpreted to her what was going on with them. Translated, that means she listened as I complained about how they refused to go into the safety and security of a retirement center, how much easier it would be for my family and my brother's family (also at a long distance from them) if they would just go and not have the responsibilities and dangers of the house and the yard. Further translated, as I am certain she has done, that meant we would be unburdened of the worry and presumed responsibility for them if we could shuffle them off to a center and be assured they were getting meals, living in a place that was

cleaned regularly and had a pull cord in every room
for when they fell.

At one point, my brother and his wife and my
family went to visit with the sole surreptitious agenda
of setting up our parents in a local retirement center
where my Dad's sister lived. They thought at first it
was a good idea and even visited several with us.
We put down a deposit on one of them and got on
our separate planes feeling successful and relieved
that the folks were now going to be in good hands.
All it would take from us would be another trip or
two to help them pack and sort through the accumulation of sixty-five years of married life together.

The next day my father withdrew the deposit,
blaming it on my mother because he knew we
wouldn't fight as much with her. They will stay in
the house until one or both dies there, as indeed
they are perfectly entitled to do.

As we went through these and other machina-
tions, I became aware of modeling for my daughter
the way to deal with aging parents, and now am
sure she will want to shuttle us off to some interga-
lactic space station for the elderly on the outer fringes
of Pluto should we live long enough to be in this
position.

At the same time as I interpreted her
grandparents and their foibles to her, from time to
time I saw my own behavior with her mirroring that
of my parents with me and sought to alter it. I told
her I disagreed with the bumper sticker that read:

"The best revenge is to live long enough to be a burden to your kids." I assured her that, unlike many people, her mother and I did not expect her to take care of us in our old age. Of course she would spend many painful hours in Hell if she didn't, but the choice really was up to her. She laughed and promised never to leave us. She is a very young thirteen and will get over that sentiment in a few months.

With parents pressing from the top and daughter pressing from the bottom, the sandwich became a vise, squeezing me with demands and responsibilities for which I felt usually unprepared, always unready, and frequently unwilling.

At forty-six I wanted more and more time to myself and alone with my wife. The problem of the plateau of the forties is the ability to see in both directions equally well - where we have been and where we are going. The problem with being sandwiched between the increasing demands of aging parents and the increasing demands of adolescent children is that the squeeze comes at the very time when we have this remarkable vision - along with a sudden acuity of hearing that counts the seconds on the time clock of our lives as though they were being announced by Big Ben.

BONG. FORTY SEVEN.
BONG. FORTY EIGHT.
BONG. FORTY NINE.
BONG. NINETY THREE.

The *external* pressures sandwich us between them just as we start to feel tremendous *internal* pressure to live our *own* lives fully, with pleasure and leisure and accomplishment and meaning. At times we feel like an exploding hot dog in a cast iron bun. For my family that is a particularly appropriate metaphor because my father worked for a meat packing company and drove a bright yellow car with a wiener on top. The hot dog on wheels that transported me to school every morning was now imploding.

Conversations with my brother changed their focus from the casual exchange of information about each other's lives and families, to discussions of the various "What if?" scenarios that could develop with our parents and what we would do when they happened. If Mom died first, what would we do with Dad - and vice versa? What if one breaks a hip or has a stroke? What if they are injured in a car accident? What if they simply became senile or physically incapable of caring for themselves or each other? What if they outlive us?

Of course speculation is silly. Although it helps us feel a sense of control in an uncontrollable situation, the truth is we won't know the right thing to do until we get there. I would do as well to speculate about various responses to my teenage daughter's daily conundrums, or to the choices she will make regarding her appearance, schoolwork, and relationships with boys.

So in fact there is nothing to *do* about the upper and lower crusts of my sandwiched life, except to acknowledge their presence and that they each have a life of their own. While I have responsibilities for each of them, I have no control over either of them.

My parents will do as much as they are able for as long as they are able, and I will support them in that endeavor until they become hazardous to themselves or each other. I can comment on their choices, but I cannot control them. I can wish they would get someone in to help clean and do the cooking and yardwork, or that they would use their accumulation of funds to pay for a retirement center where all that is covered, but I cannot dictate it. As long as they are competent, the part of their parenting role that they will rigidly defend is their right to solicit and then ignore their children's advice, which ironically puts them back into the role of the rebellious child.

Likewise, my daughter will get through her adolescence with the values that are already deep within her, testing limits in all directions as she experiences new thoughts and feelings. I can comment on her choices but I cannot, ultimately, control them. I know this from my own adolescence with my own parents, as well as from my experience with them now. She will rebel in her way, and succeed and fail and develop into a young adult with her own life and her own interests and her own loves. The best I can hope for is that we remain in communication through this period so that we might become closer friends at the end of it.

In fact, the only part of the sandwich in my control is the middle part - myself (the wrinkling hot dog.) I can use the pressures of this sandwich vise to remedy old thoughts and feelings from my lifelong interaction with my parents. Perhaps as issues are raised I can come to terms with them, even put them to rest, without reliving them and trying to finish unfinished business through my daughter.

At the same time I can deal with my own aging in more creative ways, still bouncing off the model of my parents but not trying to defend against my own aging by attempting to control theirs.

It occurs to me that maybe this is exactly what our forties are for. Perhaps the function of the sandwich vise is - on the one side - to squeeze out of us the last vestiges of our childhood issues, to force us to come to terms with what we would, if left to our own fearful security, ignore at all costs rather than dig up, relive, and confront. And - on the other side - to force us to look ahead to our own inevitable aging so that we can prepare for it in a different way than our own parents did, and by living every day in the meantime. Even as we parent our parents, we still learn from them.

No wonder people have described this period as the mid-life crazies. No wonder many of us respond to the vise grip by trying to wiggle out of it, ignore the opportunities to change and instead try to maintain the status quo and disregard the strong warnings about our future. Divorce, affairs, cashing out and moving to Maine, substance use, plastic surgery, changing jobs or partners, buying a sports car, downsizing, changing clothes style, remodeling the house or building a new one - all these are behaviors we use to work through the issues imposed on us by the squeeze of the mid-life sandwich.

In my forties I remarried, changed houses, acquired a six year old daughter, published books, ran marathons and bought a sports car. Though these have been pleasant and meaningful distractions, the sandwich vise continued to squeeze until I started to deal with the issues necessary to progress into my fifties and beyond.

Soon I will make the long trek to visit my parents again. I will listen and comment and walk the tightrope between child and parent as they, with cane and walker, negotiate the tightrope between parent and child. I will silently overlook my father's poignant comments about taking my mother on a cruise someday, knowing she can hardly negotiate her way from kitchen to bath much less bunk to deck; and I will listen sadly to my mother's wish to have her aching legs work again, and not to be so tired so often. I will also listen in awe to their schedule of outings during the week: dinners, receptions, parties, church functions and the important volunteer work at the state hospital where, at age eighty-eight,

Dad holds the office of Secretary, and they were voted volunteers of the month.

Returning home, I will hug my wife, joke with my daughter, and go for a long run by myself.

MASSAGE

When I was a kid my older brother and I got up every Saturday at 7 a.m. to watch what was called The Early Movie. We'd gaze bleary eyed through the steam of hot chocolate as Roy Rogers, Gene Autry and Hopalong Cassidy sang their way through range fights, shoot outs and "wimmin" of all descriptions.

Sometimes the t.v. station would slip in what my brother and I dubbed "Easterns" and we'd watch The Dead End Kids be falsely accused of a crime and have to get themselves out of it by finding the real criminal. Or a detective like Bogart or Mitchum with fists of iron, hearts of gold and a steel "Roscoe" in their pocket would be faced with "the puzzle of his career" and go sleazing through the underworld to find the dangerous surprise answer.

Now the difference between the Westerns and the Easterns was *massage*. The closest cowboys ever came to other flesh touching theirs was being nuzzled by their faithful horse. But the Easterns always had the hero dropping by the local downtown gym to ask some questions of "Pop" or one of the current contenders, none of whom, we noticed, seemed to have any visible means of support.

My absolute favorite Saturday morning detective was Boston Blackie, so named for his slick black hair and thin black moustache. Blackie was sort of a graduate Dead End Kid - an ex-con who went straight but was always charged with the murder. His first step in catching the bad guys was to drop by the local gym because his short, tough, sidekick worked there as a sparring partner.

At the gym some fighter was always "getting a rub down" (code word for what would later be called "massage.") And it was always done by the old blind man who once had been a great fighter himself but since "that fight" had become a "trainer" (code word for what we would later call "masseuse.") He was also the only one who seemed to work for a living, except the cops of course.

Once my brother and I thought it might be fun to imitate that trainer. We stripped off our shirts and did what we thought was "back rub down." The only impact our karate chops and fist pounding had was on our mother, who had to doctor the bruises and scratches.

It should be no surprise, then, that I would later approach the subject of "massage" with skepticism bordering on disgust. None of my heroes had done this - or allowed it to be done to them - and the only way it was to be legally accomplished was by an old blind ex-fighter who might yet pound your flesh to within an inch of hamburger meat.

This presented a problem in the late Sixties and early Seventies when "massage" took on a very different connotation. James Bond seemed to think it was okay, but it often led him to trouble with the bad guys. Marshall McCluhan elevated the word to cult status, though he was misquoted by an imprecise reporter. McCluhan actually said "The medium is the *massage*," not the *"message."*

In those years I remember walking through various shops in places like Provincetown (Cape Cod) and Greenwich Village, with the distinct impression that massage was now associated with the musky scents of body oils, incense, pot and sex. Though the first three truly never interested me, I was particularly fond of that last item and learned that the art of *sensuous* massage could prove both erotic and relaxing at the same time, oil or no oil. That was when I was twenty-five and capable of what are now inexplicable sexual gymnastics.

In my late thirties, I was no longer swinging from the chandeliers but I still found that sensual massage provided a certain amount of desired vulnerability. To gently explore with a cohabiting partner each other's textures led to a sense of knowing and being known that was the "stuff" of real intimacy. But still I could not understand why otherwise perfectly normal friends of mine would get misty-eyed and poetic about "what a *fantastic* massage" they had had that day. They referred, of course, to a perfect stranger, NOT an old blind ex-fighter (with the emphasis on the *blind*), squeezing their body parts.

The fact that this made absolutely *no* sense to me was the source of endless jokes and ridicule. I was accused of being everything from an anal retentive control freak to a typical uptight macho male, to which I countered that I was neither typical nor a freak. For a birthday present, one (alleged) friend provided me with a gift certificate for One Free Float To Relax. It was designed to be my first minuscule step toward an actual massage and was described as a chance to "get naked with no contact."

I am relatively sure that not every town had one of these outfits, but Austin, Texas (that liberal mecca of the Texan desert) in the early Eighties had three of them. This meant either that we were particularly advanced or that we needed to relax more than the inhabitants of, say, Dime Box or Cut N Shoot.

The dare was made, the gauntlet thrown down, the Free Certificate thrust into my hand - with an expiration date. To show my fearless disregard of other's opinions, I took a deep breath, relaxed my sphincters, and strode into the Float To Relax place in the late afternoon of the expiration date assuming there could not possibly be enough time to indulge. Unfortunately, they had just extended their hours and greeted me with blank stares. They had obviously never had a customer in a black shirt and clerical collar.

"What do you want?" the woman in the opaque white gauze blouse asked.

"Gift certificate," I said, not staring at her brown nipples pointing attentively in my direction.

She rose, picked up a towel and motioned me to follow her to the back room. "Have you done this before?"

Not being exactly sure what "this" referred to, I mumbled "Not *here*," and followed, lemming-like, as she explained the process.

"This is the float room." She opened the door to an eight by twelve room, just large enough to contain a waist high wooden box and a shower stall.

Motioning to the box she said, "You will see that this does *not* look like a coffin," at which point it looked like every coffin I had ever seen in my whole life. "It is filled with six to eight inches of salt water that will allow you to float with no effort at all."

Or possibly drown you in three minutes.

"You take off your clothes..."

No kidding. Why did she say that? It sounded like an invitation, especially since the clothes she had *on* appeared *off*.

"Most people like to shower first," she said, pointing to the stall and handing me the towel.

Together? Was she going to watch? Join me? Hopefully? Did she think I *needed* a shower? Or were there tiny hidden cameras that allowed her to watch from her front office to see what happened when the clerical collar was removed?

"I'll give you ten minutes to get into the tank, then I'll come in and lower the lid."

Great. I would then get to experience what the funeral directors do as I'm saying final words over the deceased in their parlors. "Okay. Then what?"

"Then you just relax. We'll be back in an hour to tell you time's up."

Both of them had to come back? It took *two* of them to unload the soggy corpse from this Poe-like structure? I nervously remembered a large dumpster where I parked my car, and envisioned the two of them on each end of a 5'10" carpet roll, my exact height.

She slapped the top of the box twice with her palm. "That will be the signal for you to come out."

Assuming I am still able. "Thank you," I said, the way the criminal thanks the hangman for the hood.

She closed the door and I looked around for hidden cameras. I was sure my friends were videotaping this event to release to the press when I won the Nobel Prize or ran for President.

I disrobed, neatly stacking my clothes with my underwear tucked inside my folded pants so there would be no embarrassment to the police when the body was found.

It was not until I was in the shower, with barely warm water dribbling out of the nozzle, that I felt *totally* stupid. Here I was, the person who reserves nudity for the privacy of his own home, standing butt-bare in a shower in a public business where an opaquely naked woman with pointy brown nipples was about to come close a lid on his watery non-coffin.

Just when was it that I had lost my sanity, I wondered? Gene Autry would not do this. Neither would Boston Blackie. Even James Bond would have some device hidden (God knows *where* at this point) to get him *out* of this situation when it got really dangerous.

There was still time to back out, I reasoned. But that would be too humiliating. I could lie to my friends and tell them it went great, but they would not only have the hidden videotape to show the truth, they could also question the proprietors (probably from a prison cell.) Besides, the woman and her male companion would think I chickened out because I'm a squeamish, prudish priest. I had to maintain for them the public image of clergy as liberal, open, risk-takers who live on the edge.

I would have to lie.

I would tell them my asthma flared. No, too easy. I would tell them that, once in the shower, I suddenly discovered a running sore on my...

Knock at the door.

Damn. I had taken too long in there. Now they would think I was doing something *else* in there.

"Wait a second," I said, lowering my voice two notches for effect. I scurried out of the shower and into the non-coffin box. The water was cool after the warm drool from the shower stall. "Okay."

To my surprise, relief - and dismay - the *man* came in and glanced through the opening. "We'll be back for you in an hour," he said as though he were talking to the Thanksgiving turkey.

I should be done by then? "Right."

He closed the lid. I heard him shut the door.

It was "The Cask of Amontillado" revisited. With my eyes wide open it was pitch black, the kind of black from which you know you will never escape.

I lay in six inches of luke-cold water, allegedly saturated with salt that was supposed to keep my head and the rest of me floating, suspended in deep space with no resistance from my muscles, allowing perfect relaxation and tranquility.

It was hell. Dante should have experienced this. It would have beefed up his descriptions.

I had not had "informed consent." Either that or I missed the sign that said "Should not be attempted by anyone with claustrophobia, weak neck muscles, or a desire to live."

It was like floating in a cesspool, except that I wasn't floating. The closest I got to "float" was that several unrelated parts of me occasionally "bobbed." A foot here, a hand there, a...never mind that.

My *head* neither bobbed nor floated. It sank. It rested on the bottom of the tank, where I imagined silt and other bodily detritus from the hundreds of persons, showered and unshowered, who had preceded me in this thing. It was slimy, like being the last one into the bath in Calcutta.

With my head on the bottom, the water level covered my eyes and ran up my nose, so I had to tense my neck muscles to keep above water. I tried locking my fingers together behind my head and that allowed me to keep my nose up, but salt or scum or something still seeped into the sides of my eyes, not to mention my ears.

How would I explain my sudden blindness and deafness to my family?

"Well, I let them lock me in this coffin-like box with year old water in it...and...yes, I was naked at the time..."

Uh-oh. Naked. That meant that my *other* orifices were subject to contact with the sewer water, to the bazillions of bacteria from other persons' private orifices who had lain here before me, and who were probably not of the North German anal retentive, fastidious, meticulous, clean-freak mentality that had kept me disease free - until *now*.

All of this ran through my mind in the first five minutes. Now I only had fifty-five more to endure the consequences and plan a strategy for recuperation.

Perhaps a broad spectrum antibiotic followed by massive doses of alcohol.

The silence and the exhaustive attempts to stay alive did allow me to think about my life. I vowed that, if I survived, I would kill my friends. Better, I would provide them with One Free Float To Relax so we could all die of the same diseases.

They should call this place "TRY To Relax." That's what I was doing, playing mind games that put me every place I had ever travelled in the world but here. I made lists of things I had to do if I got through this, like someone in an iron lung bargaining with God.

Finally, I closed my eyes (why?) and simply endured.

Out of nowhere came two loud knocks on the coffin.

KNOCK. KNOCK.

I jerked like a cow in pirhanas.

The lid opened and I popped up.

Chuck-in-a-box.

"How was it?" said the guy without the gauze woman.

"Great," I lied.

He tilted the lid open and left. I showered again in hopes of removing some of the fungi and other organisms that had taken root in my pores. On my way out I handed the woman the towel.

"Come back again," she said flatly.

Yes, I'll rush in at the first announcement of nuclear war.

"Bye."

Not long after that the place went out of business, partly due to the AIDS scare and partly due to the large number of drownings and psychotic breaks induced by being locked naked in a coffin with six inches of water and weak neck muscles.

As one might imagine, that experience resulted in a further plummeting of whatever weak interest I might have had in massage, which I equated with going one step beyond "floating."

My friends had even more difficulty explaining to me why anyone in his right mind would *voluntarily* strip naked, assume a *prone* position on a table (akin to the box) on which other bodies had previously lain naked with no protective sheet of germ free doctor's office examining table paper, and allow a perfect *stranger* to put her (or his) hands on his person.

After escaping, Houdini-like, from the Float-To-Die-Coffin, it was now even *more* repulsive to me - until I passed the age of forty and talked to my friend Steve, also an Episcopal priest.

"I thought exactly like you," he said over a beer on his back porch one afternoon. "But let me tell you what happened."

He lowered his voice so the kids would not hear.

"My wife has gotten massages for years, and she's been telling me forever I need to do this."

"Same here," I replied. "But I've gone forty-three years without one and with any luck I can survive another forty-three in the same condition."

"Yeah...but listen. Her brother gave me a free massage for my birthday last month. I was going to blow it off, let it expire, ignore it."

"Good tactics, all."

"But I didn't. I decided, what the hell, clergy are

liberal, open, risk-takers who live on the edge."

"You should have called me first. There's sure to be a Twelve Step program for this."

"So one afternoon I told the church secretary I was going to make some home visits - which was the truth, actually, because the address on this thing was a house."

"Of what...?"

"So I'm nervous as hell and I pull up in front of the house - it was an old house in the University area - and I expect to see Brunhilda at the door. I ring the doorbell and who answers but this petite, young - about 23 - co-ed, with blonde hair, blue eyes, short shorts and a tube top barely restraining its abundant contents."

"And you didn't bolt and run?"

"Chuckie, Chuckie, Chuckie. Life is short. And in your forties you know it's getting a hell of a lot shorter."

"Stevie, Stevie, Stevie. Your wife will shorten yours when she finds out."

"That's another story. Let me continue."

"Please do."

"'OH', the cutesy co-ed says, obviously moved by my handsome, suave and attractive appearance."

"Not to mention the collar."

"Not to mention the collar. She said: 'Come right in. She took the card and looked at it. 'GREAAAAAAT.' She kept flopping back her mop of blonde hair like a caricature of herself. She told me to go upstairs and get ready.

"'Up-stairs?' I asked, my pulse starting to race."

"'Yes' she said, 'I do the massage in my bed-room...'"

"My voice went soprano. 'On the bed?' I said, incredulously.

"'No, silly,' she smiled. 'On the table in there. Go ahead and use the bathroom and then get on the table, on your back. Some people prefer to leave their underpants on and..' Here she smiled and flipped her blonde mop. 'Well...others don't.'"

"And you *WENT* upstairs?" I said, somewhere between disbelief and envy.

"I gotta admit there was one moment when I thought I should head for the car and boogie." Steve smiled that goofy FDR smile of his. "But I didn't. I sat in the bathroom wondering if I should go under-wear-less or not. But I figured..."

"You figured: Why not? Clergy are daredevil, risk taking..."

"Right."

"Weren't you worried you'd...uh..."

"Worried? I was terrified. I just knew that if I hopped up on that table butt naked in that girl's bedroom and let her put her cute little co-ed hands on me that I'd raise the sail to full hoist."

"You are describing my worst nightmare."

"Let me finish. I decided to go for it. I took off my underpants and neatly put them out of sight in my folded shirt on top of the toilet."

"We are of the same gene pool. You are about to stroll stark naked into a strange, sensually attractive young woman's bedroom to let her put her hands all over your body and you take the time to fold your u-trou and hide them out of sight so nobody - especially *her* - will *see* them. There is something wrong with this picture."

"I hopped up on the table and pulled the sheet over me."

"And the thin sheet left no doubt as to your gender, right?"

"Right. She put her hands under my neck and started squeezing my tense shoulders and I thought this could work out okay. But then she said: 'Roll over.'"

"Uh-oh."

"You got it. There I was lying face down on this table with my genitals pressed upon mightily and incredibly wonderful fantasies racing through my brain propelled by my warp speed pulse, not to mention her short shorted thighs nudging against my legs and arms."

"How did you control yourself?"

"I just plain decided that I was going to enjoy the hell out of this and whatever happened, happened."

"You are certifiable."

"When she finished oiling my back she said to roll over again."

"And did we raise the sail and wave in the breeze?"

"No, we didn't." The FDR smile again. "But we came close."

"What happened?"

"She brushed by the old appendage a couple of times on the way from thigh to navel."

"By *accident*, I am certain."

"Yeah," he smiled. "Me too..."

"And that was *it*?"

"Yep. When I got back downstairs she was making tea in the kitchen. She saw me to the door and said: 'Oh, Steve, I *do* hope you'll come back again. I *really* enjoyed doing your massage. Your body is so amazingly, I don't know...*supple*.'"

"So you tipped her, naturally."

"Natch. But only five bucks. Clergy must maintain a frugal image."

"And when you arrived at your domicile, with your wife and two children awaiting you, did you enter as the king of the castle and share the joy of your recent whereabouts?"

"Are you *kidding* me?"

"But clergy are honest."

"I was honest. She asked how I was and I told her I had used the free massage certificate and she asked enthusiastically how I liked it and I said demurely, oh, it was okay, and she said did I think I'd go back and I said, oh, probably."

"Honest to a fault."

"Only one problem."

"She went to the masseuse?"

"Worse. This town is incestuously small."

"The movies?"

"Nope, supermarket."

"Oh no."

"We were in the produce section and I had two heads of lettuce in my hands when the blonde in the red tube top bounces up with her shopping cart."

"She can't buy many clothes with five dollar clergy tips. And she says to me as she passes by: 'Hi Steve! Call soon!'"

"And your wife, the charming, wonderful, understanding thing that she is, said...?"

"'Who the hell was *that*?'"

"Perfectly understandable."

"I thought so too, which is why I immediately told her the whole story."

"The truth?"

"Unembellished."

"Which was?"

"That the woman was a professional in every way. And that I kept my shorts on."

"Which was, of course, the truth until you entered the bathroom."

"Right."

"And the future of you and the masseuse?"

"No future, only history. My wife got on the phone to my brother-in-law and shared with him the depth of her appreciation for his gift."

"So your brother-in-law can't go back again, either?"

"Brilliant, my dear Holmes."

"Thank you, brother Steven, for further enhancing my phobia and deepening my prejudice against the fine art of massage. I'm afraid I *still* don't get it."

"Actually," he finally confessed, "...me neither. It was a fun story, but I probably wouldn't go back."

"Because clergy are control-freaks?"

"Nah. Costs too much and all you get to do is lay there."

"'Lie' there."

"Right," Steve grinned. "All lies and no lays."

But my forties marched on, and with the marching the sound of that distant massage-drummer got louder.

Is it that our forties provide us with perspective that results in greater security so we are *free* to attempt new things, perhaps things we may not have considered in younger years? Or, looking in the opposite direction, do we begin to see that there may not be quite so many years up ahead so we had better get on with the things we had the luxury of avoiding earlier?

Whichever is the case (probably a bit of both), a few more years found me at mid-45 with a trip to Northern California in the offing. My wife and I had plans to stay in a nice B&B on the ocean in Mendocino. Because my otherwise quite sane spouse is, like many of my otherwise sane friends, an avid consumer of the art, she asked if the place offered massage. When I called, the owner indicated the locals offered any kind of massage I could imagine, along with acupuncture, Chi Gong, and a menu of assorted New Age treatments that made massage sound conservative and old fashioned.

The time seemed right. California was the land of body-glomming. Browsing brusquely or lazily grazing over the skin of another person was as routine as traffic jams and earthquakes, as common as pet cemeteries, channeling, and wineries. It was not like Texas, where the deer and antelope play but not with each other's bodies and where "massage" still carries jaded connotations of commie-pinko-radical-carpetbagging-Yankees or their moral equivalent - people from Colorado.

In Mendocino the moment came when my wife had just gotten off the phone with the masseuse, a local woman who knew the B&B owner and brought a table right to your room. I was lounging on the couch, wife in my arms, gazing into the crackling fireplace, working on my third glass of a local Cabernet Sauvignon.

"I've been thinking about this massage business," I announced bravely, "...a lot. My only problem is that it is probably too expensive, so..."

"She told me that she'll do 'two-fers'."

"Must be a *big* table..."

My wife looked at me as she would our twelve year old daughter. "One at a time."

I pondered this through two more sips of wine.

"The other one *watches*?"

Monotone response: "The other one goes up to the pool and boils in the jacuzzi."

"Makes sense to me."

"You going to do it?"

More pondering. More wine. "Why not?" I said. "Clergy are..."

"...Liberal, open, risk takers who live on the edge."

"Thank you."

The next morning I ran six miles after breakfast to tire out my body. I figured if I was already exhausted when I got on the table I wouldn't be as tense, and therefore wouldn't be worrying about raising the sail in the middle of the massage.

It was decided that I would go first. My wife knew if I left the room she'd have trouble finding me later. I drank a beer waiting around for the knock at the door, like a kid waits in the dentist's office for an extraction. I sat on the balcony overlooking the ocean and drank another beer. I was plenty relaxed and decided I didn't really *need* a massage, what with all the beer and running, but my petite, karate-expert wife was between me and the door. I went back to the balcony.

The whole time I wondered what she'd look like, this woman who "brought her table to your room." What if she looked like the one that did Steve? Hell, I could always back out, tell my wife I preferred the pool and jacuzzi and spend the rest of my life living this down.

Prayer is important at these times, as all clergy know. "Please, please let her look like the old, blind, ex-fighter. In fact, let her *be* the old, blind ex-fighter."

Knock at the door. A *loud* knock. This person had biceps.

Another knock. The sound was amazingly like the one on the non-coffin Float To Relax box. I hoped the massage table would *not* look like a coroner's slab.

I opened the door to find neither a cutesy co-ed nor the old, ex-fighter. This woman was dressed in the standard California baggy cotton pants and shirt, shoulder length dark hair clipped up on her head, with a slightly anorexic build that bulged in places I wished mine did.

"Hi. I'm Sharon."

"Need any help setting up?" Dumb question. If *she* couldn't lift something, *I* sure couldn't.

Fortunately for me, Sharon was a very relaxed, calm, unassuming person who could just as easily have been a potter or an elementary school teacher - until she got warmed up on the table, at which time she turned into Bruce Lee.

"Who's first?"

"I'm going up to the pool," my wife said, smiling her way out the door. "See you in an hour and a half."

"An hour and *a half*?" I smiled back through clenched teeth. I had psyched myself up for an *hour* of endurance at this task. Now I would be trapped here with this complete stranger for *ninety* minutes. "Thanks for telling me, *dear*."

Door closed, Sharon starts explaining.

"You have to tell me how hard you want me to do it and how deep you want me to go."

I am a *very* literal person. This was getting off to a bad start.

"I am a runner," I announce in as baritone a voice as I can muster, as though this sound will explain a certain invincibility to pain. "Hard and deep."

"Some people leave their underwear on, so I don't do buttocks or abdomen, or off and I do both."

I nod, nonchalantly, as though this trivial information is wasting our precious time. "Off," I say confidently, my baritone slipping close to soprano. "We'll do the whole enchilada."

Bad choice of words on my part, I know.

"I'll leave the room and come back in a few minutes."

I don't get this. I know it seems thoughtful of her to grant me privacy while I'm getting naked under the sheet - but does anyone in this state (all of whom are probably watching the video as we speak) really think that she's not going to *see the goods* when she comes back in the room and looks *under* the sheet?

Knock at the door.

Flashback to Die-To-Relax coffin.

"Come in."

She closes the door. It's happening. I'm doing this thing I said I'd never do. But I'm forty-five and counting. Besides, clergy are...

"Roll over."

Arf. I lay with my face in what appears to be a catcher's mitt with the center cut out so I could see the floor and her naked, sandal-less, muscular feet pushing against the floor as she moves around my body. The crown jewels are squashing dangerously against my inner thighs.

"Oil?"

"Sure." Flashbacks of Greenwich Village.

She starts at my feet and it actually feels kind of good.

"That too hard?"

No, I wanted to quit walking anyway. "Fine." Maybe pain will take my mind off of the sensation that is growing in my groin. "Perhaps a bit deeper."

This is great. Feet are at the far end of the body. Maybe I can get her to take so much time down there that she won't have time to work her way into the center.

Suddenly she finishes the feet. She is a professional. Undeterred by my schedule, she will cover every inch of my body before we are through or her job is not done. And, thanks to my charming and crafty spouse, she has an hour *and a half* to do it in.

The sheet is pulled back, modestly revealing the right half of my lower rear torso. I cannot see this, obviously, but along with the other competing images racing through my mind, I envision that my right butt is exposed to the breeze and she's *got* to be gazing at whatever items might be viewed below it.

She takes long, sweeping strokes with her iron hands up my leg, with forays into my inner thigh. Then she kneads my right bun like a loaf of bread, manually noting the tight muscles and giving them deeper attention.

Meanwhile back at the ranch, I suddenly know why Gene Autry never did this, and why the old, blind ex-boxer was so well employed. It occurs to me, amidst rapid forays between my thighs and excavations into my gluteus maximus, that the only time I have been naked and touched by a woman was as a child (by my mother) and during sensual encounters with Significant Others. This was the *first time*, at age forty-five, that I lay naked and vulnerable, allowing a complete stranger of the female persuasion to run her oily hands over my tight runner's buns with absolutely *no goal, no ulterior motive, no control, and no reciprocation.*

It was bizarre. Why hadn't I thought of this before? Why hadn't I connected this great insight? I was totally unprepared for the revelation. It was absurd. And the only thing I could think of doing was - to laugh.

Now you do *not* laugh when you are under the thumbs of a woman of her muscle power, for fear that she may take offense and cripple you for life. So I laughed *internally*, inside my mind, smiling through the catcher's mitt at her feet on the floor.

She did the other leg and bun, with dangerously close swipes at the jewels. By this time, however, the humor had taken the edge off the eroticism and I was actually beginning to enjoy having my muscles kneaded and pounded by Sharon, who was, behind the closed eyes of my mind, really the old, blind fighter with great hands and no memory (not to mention sight.)

Then came the words I had forgotten I dreaded: "Turn over."

It was a softly spoken command and one I'd heard before. In those instances I knew where I stood (or laid), I knew and anticipated with great joy what the next step would be, and I looked forward to reciprocating in a similar manner.

Not now.

Now I was dreading the movement of hands nearer and nearer the most vulnerable part of my body. Now I was fearing the sudden arousal of that part. I could see it all in my mind and it was not a pretty sight. She finished my feet and moved up my legs. And it turned out she *was* a professional. She didn't even come close to nicking or brushing the jewels.

A year later the hour and a half was up and Sharon took her bony, muscular feet out of the room while I jumped off the table, slipped on my swim trunks and waited for my wife to return.

She did, smile still intact on her pretty face, already anticipating the reverie she would experience at the hands of this female Adonis.

"Well...how did you *like* it?"

It was the most stressful ninety minutes of my life. "Greeeaaaaaatttt," I lied, convincingly. "We'll talk about it later." Smooched her on the forehead. "I'll be back in an hour and a half," I said, as Sharon reappeared at the door, ready to do battle with yet another set of hardened, stress locked muscles which would first resist her plying, then give way to her healing touch with suppleness and comfort.

My muscles, on the other hand, were supremely grateful to be untouched by strange human hands. They were, to be honest, more relaxed, but I am sure that had more to do with the fact that the massage was *over* than with the fact that it had *occurred*.

As I sat in the jacuzzi and ruminated on the experience (as they say in California) I couldn't wait to get back to tell Steve and all my skeptic friends that I had actually *done it*. I had had a massage and *survived* to tell the tale.

I would not do it again. I still don't see the point. It is one of those things you should *choose* to do before you're fifty and *have* to have a massage by a physical therapist upon a written order from your physician. That sort of takes the adventure out of it, at least for us clergy who are liberal, risk taking, etc.

Massage, in my humble, Germanic, anal retentive, control freak opinion, is for women (or Californians) who revel in such passive bodily activity. It is certainly not a part of the Texas cowboy, Gene Autry, Roy Rogers picture which provided me so many meaningful role modeled hours as a child. The only way I might consider repeating the experience is if I could find that old, blind man from the gangster movies of my kidhood who would, with no sexual overtones, no sensuality, and no goal of relaxation, pummel my muscles into submission in the traditional masculine manner, reducing my body to the consistency of jello in a socially acceptable way.

Until I find that person, and I am not looking very hard for him, I will continue to run three times a week and endure (with the ears of an experienced victim) the misty-eyed stories of my wife and others as they wax poetic on the results of their *fantastic* massage.

And no one will rub me the wrong way.

HAIRCUT

I was more than surprised, I was shocked. I prefer to see myself as well educated (watches Masterpiece Theatre,) progressive (wants national healthcare,) and socially benevolent (drives for Meals on Wheels.) But I am embarrassed to say that a recent experience called forth in me responses that can only be categorized as Neanderthal. Something happened that evoked emotions, prejudices, and stereotypes so deeply rooted in my psyche that no amount of therapy over the years has been able to loosen the grasp of their tightly wound tendrils from my cerebral cortex.

It was about this haircut.

It is not exactly - as my 11 year old daughter keeps reminding me - that I have a lot of hair to cut. In fact, as I enter my late forties, I look more and more like my father and grandfather, both of whose hairlines receded to somewhere north of Fargo. The blessing in this genetic curse is that I spend less on haircuts than most of my friends, because I go less often than they do.

This time I had waited too long. Since I do some public speaking, I note on my pocket calendar to go to my favorite barber shop three days before a major presentation. Everyone knows it takes three days for your haircut to look right.

A busier than usual schedule had repeatedly postponed the trip to the barber. I looked shaggy. The hair on my neck tufted over my shirt collar, wet hair after a shower protruded straw-like over my ears, the odd long eyebrow stuck up like one of those weird caterpillar hairs. I was certain my blank calendar showed no major public events (other than work) so I assumed that I could hold off just a little longer until the weekend.

I had already pictured it in my mind. Get up Saturday morning, put coffee in a go-cup and drive across town to be there shortly after they opened. Solitude at that hour, just me, the smell of the coffee and the hum of the car, on our way to do something relaxing and pleasurable and known. It's interesting how, as we age, the known becomes comforting and the comforting becomes enticing.

I would park and walk to the shop, read the Saturday paper and check for movies as I waited for the first chair to be ready, listen to the chatter of the barbers and the customers enjoying the slowness of the early morning together, as men rise from camp to drink coffee and sit by the fire.

Called by name - welcomed, really - I would advance almost reverently to the soft, cracked, blue leather chair with the stainless steel frame. As a kid, I remember thinking it was a combination teeter totter and throne; big enough for Ol' King Cole to sit his merry old soul upon, yet capable of doing strange things - moving up and down like a carousel pony, and swiveling around like a stool at the dime store lunch counter. Unlike the rest of the technological world, these barber chairs would never progress into modern, sleeker models. Like those hovering around them with scissors and those of us sitting in them, the chairs just got older.

Once I was comfortably seated, a striped cape would be ceremoniously shaken out. Real barbers made it sound like the crack of a whip, that call to order before the snipping began. And always there remained on the cape a few clipped hairs from the preceding person to indicate the intermingling of our male community. The cape would be tied around the little paper tissue at my neck; secure, but not tight. The tissue was placed there, undoubtedly, to differentiate the cape from a bib, which it was. Then someone I knew and trusted would ask the same questions they always asked: "Just a trim, right? Maybe a little off the top? Get those eyebrows for ya?"

The barber would position the chair with a couple of loud pumps on that lever at the side. He'd make sure I faced toward the corner of the shop, where I could glance up at the color t.v. next to the deer head, or join in conversation with other customers, or just sit and do nothing, maybe close my eyes a little, relax and be part of the scenery.

All kinds of people came into that shop. The entertainment was always some little kid there for his first or second haircut. The four barbers, Joe, John, Cliff and Albert, noticeably slow down when his Dad brings him in. You can see the four of them caught, trapped in the tension between seeing the kid as a future customer - fresh young hair that will grow voluminously and need cutting weekly for years - and seeing him as a whiny screaming pain in the ass that you want to sedate for fifteen minutes like a vet does a cat.

Eventually, one of the barbers - somehow it is usually John - has to stop pretending to get the one last out-of-place hair on his customer's sideburn, and welcomes the kid with a big smile onto the old plywood board they place across the big arms of the throne chair. The Dad holds the screaming kid's hands down while John deftly makes quick swipes at the bobbing wispy strands of thin child hair, praying he doesn't impale the kid and lose the shop to an insurance suit.

This is better than t.v. for everyone else. We watch, smile and know John will pull it off without a hitch. He always does. Watching John wield the scissors is like watching The Babe lift the bat and point to the right field fence.

The "everyone else" consists of an obviously disturbed but just as obviously accepted Vietnam veteran in a torn shirt, flak jacket and loosely tied boots, a couple of old men from the neighborhood who come in every Saturday for an unneeded trim, and various others, a student, a young professional, a cowboy or two, an hispanic worker, and another dad with an even smaller son. There is also Leon, the ninety-two year old man who shines your shoes for $1.50 and sweeps the floor between shines.

"Shine 'em *up!*" he hollers like a beer vendor at a ball park. "*Shine* 'em up!" As if everyone were as deaf as he is.

We're all there, sitting around, four of us in the throne chairs, the rest against the wall talking football, hunting and politics, commenting on the inanity of the t.v., flipping through old magazines (no Playboys, this is a family shop), reading the paper or getting a shine. It's a male place. We're not bonding or crying or beating drums, or hugging each other in sweat lodges, we're just sitting there doing the last male thing left in the culture and enjoying the hell out of it, quietly of course.

But the familiar image I dreamily anticipated was not to take place. My vacant calendar had lied about my lack of commitments. So I was not prepared for the call from my boss to remind me of the mandatory Board reception that night at the country club. One look in the mirror and I knew I had to leave work early to get shorn. As I pulled up to the shop, I remembered they were closed on Mondays, so I drove away and stopped at the first haircut place I could find.

That was my next mistake, settling for a haircut place instead of a barber shop. But I was desperate, and, being a writer, I figured I needed to have this experience.

I was wrong.

I should have trusted my instincts. My instincts looked at the "menu" of services taped to the door of the "styling salon" and told me in a voice like a car alarm - I was going to get ripped off for thirteen dollars and hate every minute of it. My instincts are always, repeat *always*, right, and I know it.

I went in anyway.

I don't care what's politically correct. The girls at the desk were girls. If they were nineteen they were elderly. They looked anorexic and wore jeans so tight they couldn't fart. They had long, fake red fingernails with chipped polish, and smoker's breath.

"Hello. Have you been to our salon before?"

If I had, do you think I'd be back? "No."

"Then we'll need you to fill this out."

A form was thrust onto the counter before me, with minuscule under-twenty writing on it. At first I thought it was a disclaimer, like a surgery permit that tells you one of the side effects of this procedure may be death, but that it's okay with you anyway.

"My name and address?" I asked sheepishly, not wanting to offend anyone prematurely, before I had entrusted my few remaining hairs to them. "You need this for me to get a haircut?"

"It's for our birthday club. You get a free one on your next birthday."

"My daughter thinks I won't *need* one on my next birthday..." I mumbled as I wrote my name and a totally fictitious address and phone. It was the phone of a whorehouse (politically correct name: modeling studio) next to where I worked.

"Just take a seat, and the next available stylist will be with you."

"Stylist?" Had she taken a good look at my head?

I knew I was in further trouble when I didn't recognize any of the magazines on the chairs. Did people really *dress* like that? On what planet?

I nervously sat glaring at the fourteen "style stations" with victims already in tow. The "stylists" all had the same black pullover polo with the company logo - an undefinable object that looked like a tiny skull and crossbones - on the left chest. For some of the people who were of the female persuasion that meant the left breast which ranged in size from Hershey's Kiss to watermelon, and in either case was unbridled.

I got neither Kiss nor melon.

I got Julio, who was probably male. His hair was short, curly, and hung over his fat neck, cleverly coordinated with the rest of his corpulence. It was one thing to have a redneck barber with a well earned barbecue-and-beer-belly comfortably cinched by a rodeo belt buckle; it was another to have Julio's mid section flabbing out under the black polo like melting cheese over his ineffectual licorice whip of a belt.

"I'm Julio. I'll be your stylist." He thrust out his sweaty hand for me to shake.

I'm Chuck. I'll be your victim. "Yeah, okay," I replied, stupidly. His hand was cold, clammy, the hand of someone near dead from melting obesity; the weak, flabby flesh of uncertainty that was about to touch, of all things, my person.

Like a drugged idiot, I followed him to "the station." He pointed to an insipid wuss of a chair with a microscopic naugahyde seat, no padding, and a foot rest like a bird perch, for small birds. My shoes kept slipping off of it, unlike the firm steel grating of my barber's throne chair with the equally firm manufacturer's name "KOKER" initialed in the middle of it. I always thought that was the sound the chair made when the barber pumped that handle to raise me up higher. KOKER. KOKER. KOKER. "That high enough for ya?" This perch-chair faced a mirror so I could see myself and, God help us, Julio doing his number. I wanted to see neither and I was nauseated anticipating what would follow.

It was worse than I imagined. They should hand out barf bags with the preflight instructions at the desk.

"I'll need you to come over to the other side to wet you down."

"Uh-huh," I said, wondering what in the world he meant. Wet me down? I did not like the connotations. I followed, zombie-like, to an area encased in plastic, like my aunt's living room in 1958.

"Sit here and put your head back in the sink." It sounded like orders from the French Revolution. I imagined Madame LaFarge looking on, knitting.

I obeyed, to see what would happen. I am certain this is how people in government experiments act, too disbelieving to question. Or maybe laboratory rats. "Oh, what the hell," they think, poking their little wet noses up to the two million volt electrode, "...how bad could it be?"

He sprayed my head with spit-warm water and ran his puffy hands through my scalp. I felt like Lon Chaney on a bad night. My thin strands of hair were matted like an old dog in the rain, where you can see the black and pink skin underneath.

"Back to the other chair," fat Julio directed.

Yes, master. I went. My brain was mush. Everything focused on survival. I would endure to get out the door and never, never, submit to this humiliation again.

"What do we want today?" he asked as I tentatively attempted to perch in the impossible chair.

WE want an Oouzi and a clear path to the door. "Just a haircut, a plain old regular run-of-the-mill haircut," I said. I knew it would throw him.

It did.

Clearly they had not covered this in hair school. Julio left for a quick consult with the Kisses at the next station and returned with a dangerously determined look on his lumpy face. He carefully divided my sopping head into four parts, like the four points of the compass, the Jungian quaternary, the Trinity plus Mary. Very spiritual, this Julio. He grabbed the strands of hair in each quadrant, pulled them up in a wad, and clipped off one one thousandth of an inch, or whatever appeared over the edge of his pudgy fingers, which wasn't much.

This technique was for poodles, not people. I wondered if he'd been trained at Bark 'N Cut?

The scissors he used were just like the blunt tips from kindergarten, except these were smaller, like nail scissors. His finger and thumb barely fit through the holes. His hand dwarfed the scissors and got in the way of cutting the hair.

In my real barbershop you can hear the gentle, rhythmic sound of snipping from four chairs at once. Real barbers, in real white barber shirts to remind us that they are, in fact, medical professionals, learn to keep the scissors snipping like electric hedge shears moving in and out to get the straggling stems of hair.

The Sesame Street Scissors did not snip. They gnawed, like an old man gumming a chicken leg. Fat Julio used them to gnaw across the few strands of wet hair that managed to struggle above the strangulation hold on their peers. He cut the hair - both elbows in the air and his tongue slightly protruding through his clenched lips, beads of sweat forming on his wrinkled forehead - as though he were clipping a coupon from the Sunday paper, on the dotted line, one strand at a time.

Gnaw. Gnaw. Gnaw.

The severed wet hair fell like dead soldiers.

"Do you want the sideburns raised?" I thought he asked.

At my barbershop the sideburn/neck shaver makes a comfortable, buzzing sound. It's vibrations massage the back of your neck while getting all those tiny, annoying neck hairs wonderfully trimmed to subcutaneous levels without ever hurting the skin. The long cord is always in the way of the barber, so he has to turn around, dance-like, or shift the shaver from hand to hand, a kind of male ritual movement akin to hiking up your pants, checking your wallet, or clenching your jaw muscles. Applying the shaver to neck and sideburns is a final sign of neatness, a message that everything is now in place as it should be, the signal to the customer that all else has been done and he can start thinking about the tip.

What I did not understand was that Julio did not mean "raised" - he meant "razed." I should have gotten the idea when he removed a white, pencil thin "shaver" from a rechargeable stand. It looked as though it was used to shave Barbie's legs.

He squinted a few inches from my temple and applied the leg shaver. In a second my sideburns were gone, demolished, pale skin fading into my ears where hair used to delineate them from my face.

"That's fine," I lied, desperate to escape further disfigurement.

When my barber puts the shaver down, he clips a couple more times, checks for clandestine ear and nose hairs, then, with another "KOKER" pump on the lever, swivels the chair around to look into the huge mirror. I nod "Great!" which is the most emotion allowed by federal law to be displayed in such an establishment. Then, and this is the really incredible part, in one facile movement too smooth for a man his size which makes it all the more magical, he turns me around, loosens the neck tissue and, like Valentino's cape, swoops the apron up and off without dropping one hair on me. A quick blast of the blower, in case any clippings have secreted themselves on my shirt, and I'm up from the KOKER throne chair and handing Joe ten dollars at the old cash register. Joe will politely hand me two dollars and I will hand him a dollar back for which he says "Thank you very much and come back," and I reply "You bet. See you in a few weeks." It is all part of the ritual.

Not so with Julio. After rearranging the roadmap of my head with interstates where there used to be redwoods, he grabbed a pink hand mirror, which came from Barbie's Bilious Bedroom, and handed it to me, the handle still wet with his sweat. The perch, of course, did not swivel, so I held the mirror behind me and looked forward into the larger mirror to see that he had cut the hair at my neckline into a Howdy Doodie, Charlie McCarthy SQUARE BLOCK.

My patience was thinning worse than my hair

_____

and it showed in my voice.

"Round the corners," I whispered through clenched teeth, Clint Eastwood-like, my breath taken away at the sight, knowing everyone at the reception tonight would be staring at the back of my head as though I had MADONNA SUCKS TOES etched into it.

The Barbie leg shaver chewed at the corners, raising the hairline nearly to that of the nonexistent sideburns. I felt like Moe.

Julio lifted the apron, spilling wet clumped hairs all over me. He looked as if it was my fault for sitting there in the first place.

It was.

He poured what appeared to be talcum powder onto a long whisk brush and swept it over my neck. I supposed this to be a limp attempt at shaving it, which he never did, so that the unruly neck hairs which had prompted this ordeal in the first place still hunched over my collar, only now they were noticeably white with powder. Nice touch.

"Come back and see us again real soon," he dripped.

When hell freezes over. "Yeah," I replied, and bolted for the girl at the desk.

Julio followed and handed her the paper with the whorehouse phone number on it. He penciled a check beside WASH AND CUT.

"Was everything satisfact'ry?" The girl said the last word in four syllables, between gum chews, like a '20's phone operator.

"Yeah," I said, wondering *when* Julio had washed my hair, and *why* anyone would 1. let someone else wash their hair in the first place since you did it every night in the shower yourself and 2. why you let anyone wash your hair BEFORE you got it cut since the purpose of washing it afterwards was to get all the little hair clippings out. I wondered if "wet you down" was the moral equivalent of "wash your hair"?

"Cash or credit card?"

Are you kidding? "Cash."

"That's thirteen dollars."

Rip off. "Here it is." I'm out of here.

"Thank you. We'll be calling you on your birthday for a free haircut."

Tell the Madame hello for me. "Great."

I strode out the door knowing I would supply all manner of conversation for them for days to come. I felt free, like Cagney stepping through prison gates to freedom after twenty five years inside, like Dante out of Purgatorio, like a child waking from a bad dream. Except that in my dream I had managed to meet Indian Julio who had scalped me before sending me to a cocktail reception where all my friends would want to know if I got the name of the truck.

Like a kid writing twenty five times on the blackboard of my mind, I said:

"I will never go to a haircut place again."

"I will never go to a haircut place again."

And:

"I will only go to my safe, sane barber for a haircut."

"I will only go to my safe, sane barber for a haircut."

Which is what I did two weeks later. I walked inside, past the familiar revolving barber pole, and sat down, aware that Joe was glancing at me, knowing he knew I had gone somewhere else in the interim, knowing he knew *where* I had gone and was restraining his snickering to save my dignity.

He motioned me to the throne chair.

KOKER. KOKER. KOKER.

"Can you fix this?" I asked.

"Sure thing," he said. "A little off the top? Get those eyebrows for ya?"

I relaxed and closed my eyes, pleasantly engulfed in the clipping, buzzing conversation. I wondered if, somehow, these feelings were archetypal.

I was glad to be home.

A GOOD DEATH

The death rate on this planet is 100 percent.

One out of one dies.

These facts were a big surprise to me when I went to work at St. David's Hospital in Austin, Texas. I was 31 and had spent ten years working in a New York penitentiary and a Texas jail, where the population was relatively young and the very few people who died on the premises were overdoses or suicides. I counted three in all that time.

I was the first chaplain the hospital had ever had. I started the job thinking people generally went to the hospital to have surgery, recover from illness, deliver a baby, and go home. By the end of the first month I had experienced fifteen deaths and wondered what I had gotten myself into.

These were not just old people whose bodies had worn out from age and illness. Most were under sixty, some neonates and stillborns. It turned out that the people who wanted to see the Chaplain were not the ones recovering from simple surgery or celebrating an uncomplicated birth. The patients needing pastoral care, along with the nurses and doctors who treated them, were the ones with serious conditions, terminal illness, and those who were dying as their helpless families looked on in sorrow and disbelief.

I was not prepared for this. I come from a family with German steel genes which, along with vast amounts of beer, whiskey, sausage and cigarettes, sustain them far up into their nineties. My parents are both in their late eighties and spend more time partying and playing cards than I do, and my diet is better.

By the time I started working at the hospital, I had known of only five deaths in my family, three of which were very elderly grandparents. Now people were dropping like flies and I was expected to know what to do to help them and their grieving families.

I was extremely fortunate to have nurses who had done this for years teach me everything they knew. From adult and neonatal intensive care to labor and delivery, from cardiology to oncology, the nurses, especially the old ones, took me aside and gave direction. I also listened carefully as patients and families taught me about what was helpful and what was not, what death meant and how they faced it, how they grieved and how they rewove the tapestries of their lives. The rest I improvised.

The 4West oncology unit was the major cauldron in which I daily percolated along, stirred by seasoned staff who were my age or younger but had done this for more years than I had. With their irreverent guidance and my own propensity toward bizarre humor, I quickly developed the kind of MASH mentality that sustained me through the daily bombardment of bodies.

It's not that death was funny. Quite the opposite. We quickly became attached to many of the families and their loved ones, learned their habits and preferences and family traditions, who to let in and who to keep out, who we could joke with and who we could not. I did a lot of funerals and still stay in touch with many of the survivors from those days.

Death was not funny - it was *ludicrous*. The things that were said or done by patients and families, the mistakes that were made by all of us, the stupid things visitors and relatives said - all made it seem like I worked on the set of "I Love Lucy To Death."

- The old lady who wore a red garter to surprise her doctor when he came to examine her.

- The young woman who wheeled herself down the hall singing "Happy Birthday to me. I'm gonna die of cancer."

- The nurse who walked in on a prostitute in bed with a young man, whose parents had provided her for him.

- The short, frumpy lady whose purse was as big as she was.

- The 300 pound woman who, when her mother died, ran screaming down the hall toward a construction door that led to four floors of thin air.

(We got her in time.)

- The housekeeper who consistently mopped floors at visiting times and aimed for staff with the buffer.

- The patient who got a staff member to scatter her ashes on the grounds of the castle in Germany where she had always wanted to go.

- The lady who was buried facing Neiman-Marcus with her credit cards in her hand. (The origin of "Don't leave home without it?")

Death became ludicrous to me at two levels: 1. the seeming cultural presumption that it should not happen, that it was immoral, unethical, bad, wrong, and optional for the human race; and 2. that people who knew better, physicians, nurses, families, clergy, acted to reinforce those notions.

My wife and I already believed in living as though life was short. Her father and grandfather had both died very young and she was intent on doing things (like traveling) without putting them off to an old age that might not be there. The stories I brought home daily only served to underscore those beliefs in both of us. Not having kids, we did the things we wanted to do basically when we wanted to do them; travelled, went to movies, stayed home and read or wrote in front of the fireplace, went to hear music, visited little festivals in small Texas towns. As it turned out, it was a good thing.

I had been at the hospital two and a half years. Deb got sick with a virulent infection and died in five days. We were thirty-four.

It was awful, but not as awful as it would have been without the death experience I had acquired by that time. For her to die was horribly unexpected but, given what I knew, not unusual. It was tragic, indelibly affecting my life and the lives of dozens of our friends, family and colleagues, but it was not unnatural.

As I slowly and painfully moved through bereavement like an ant through molasses, and lectured more around the country on death and grief issues, I put the pieces together into a book, *SURVIVING DEATH: A PRACTICAL GUIDE TO CARING FOR THE DYING AND BEREAVED.* Interestingly enough, all but three of the chapters had been written before Deb's death.

Regardless of how well *prepared* I may have been for the loss by the numbers and experience of death I had had, I was not *ready* for it. My identity was shattered, my married life suddenly stamped out. At an age when we were still on the upswing of professional, economic and emotional security, all three were gone with the person I had known since eighth grade.

The next six years were a roller coaster ride of emotions and experiences. As I daily dealt with dying people at the hospital, all my beliefs about death continued to be confirmed. Given the wonders of modern technology, there are many things that are a lot worse than death. Long term suffering, permanent vegetative states, the economic strain and often ruin of trying to provide healthcare with little or no insurance coverage, the further burdening of weakened, struggling bodies already assaulted by the debility of illness with the indignities of needles, medicines, tubes, machines, and restricted visiting hours.

For those who see the number of deaths that I do, and participate with families in these losses, death becomes a normal part of life, part of what we do here together. It's not that death loses its impact or becomes no longer tragic for those closest to it, but it is no longer shocking, surprising, or abnormal, something to be fought at all costs as if it were the evil enemy. To the contrary, death is often a form of healing, release from suffering; the normal, expected outcome of illness, accident or injury.

At first I thought one of the things worse than death was being single. Like many people my age, I had gone from parents to college to marriage. Although I had had summers of living alone or with a group of friends, I never had the sense of loneliness that I now experienced. It wasn't her death, but her absence that was devastating.

My personal situation, then, presented a small contradiction - I hated being single, and I hated dating. Like Meg's great kitchen monologue in The Big Chill, I had the routine down. I could tell in the first thirty seconds - on the phone - whether this would work out or not.

After six years of relationships that didn't, I was struck with the revelation that I might very well live the rest of my life alone. I was thirty-nine, approaching the big four-o at a reasonable running speed and imagining what fifty to sixty more years of single life might look like. Because of what my alleged friends call my stubborn bull-headedness and extensive idiosyncracies, it was not a pretty picture, especially for them.

But I found, to my surprise, that I had become comfortable with being single. I pretty much had the routine of my life down to a manageable system, and I was actually beginning to enjoy the prospect of continuing it that way, barring unforseen difficulties.

The unforseen difficulty arrived in my office one afternoon wanting to do volunteer work with cancer patients. She was single (with a six year old daughter), was equally comfortable with her life, resigned to being alone, and didn't want her equilibrium upset either. Her name was Debi, so I would have no difficulty remembering it, and she was almost three years out (the "cure" date) from a bone marrow transplant for leukemia.

Friends went nuts when we announced our marriage plans. Their concern was that I would end up facing the death of another wife, and that she would end up leaving not only a daughter but a husband. But they forgot to whom they were talking. Here was a woman who had personally faced not only her own death but what she often described as worse - the incredible onslaught of pain and debility associated with the transplant procedure and its aftermath. And here was a man who had survived the death of a spouse and saw death, his own included, as inevitable and unpredictable. What made people think that it was "safe" to marry someone who appeared to be disease free? The truth is that any of us could be diagnosed terminally ill next week, or have a stroke, or be killed in an accident, or murdered. Had they forgotten that the death rate is 100 percent?

What was (and still is) amazing to me is that people thought that we could somehow avoid pain by not marrying; that it would be better for us both and for the daughter. But the truth is that life is not a choice of pain versus no pain. It is a choice of which pain you prefer. I could choose the pain of remaining single, without a companion to share whatever life was left for us; or I could choose the pain of possibly having another person I loved die before I did, should the leukemia recur.

Those who cautioned our marriage must have believed that 1. death can be avoided if you make careful choices and don't spend time around people with illness, 2. people with cancer always die sooner than people who think they don't have it, and 3. I'd be hell to live with if this happened again. Debi and I both disagreed with the first two and I could be hell to live with whether or not she died first, so we married.

We believed then, as we believe now, that life is uncertain. The truth is that there are no guarantees of anything, especially lifespan. We were willing to take whatever risk people perceived there was to spend whatever time we had together as a couple and a family, whether that was five years or fifty years. Life together was better than life alone, damn the torpedoes, full speed ahead. Live with no regrets, or as few as possible. Being together was better than being alone.

We married two weeks after I turned forty. Three months later she relapsed. Doom and gloom prophets clucked their tongues and said "Told you so." "Shouldn't have done it." "Should have stuck with the smart money and successfully avoided her imminent death."

That was six years ago, and she's still very much alive. At the time of this writing, so am I. In the meantime, we have been to Europe four times (once on the Concorde), vacationed at least once a year, brought our daughter to the doorstep of adolescence, and buried four close friends who were not sick when we got married. Although medical tests and treatments have been difficult at times, neither of us would have chosen differently.

I have been extremely lucky to love and be loved deeply. I also began to learn unusually early (in my thirties) what I have had confirmed in my forties, that death is a normal part of life, not to be sought nor feared, but to be seen in the broader perspective of who we are and what we do here together.

I think that perspective is often only reached in our forties, from the plateau of mid-life. We look back on the achievements and failures of the first forty years with the self-satisfied feeling of having endured them all. And we cast a glance forward to the other side of the plateau knowing in a way that we did not know earlier that death is inevitably up ahead.

But there is another problem for us. As we begin to think more explicitly about it, we are very likely to be faced with the issue of how to arrange a *good death*. There is considerable interest in this as the generation that has gotten used to getting what it wants approaches retirement and old age. Given our propensity toward assertiveness, we are not likely to take death lying down.

Particularly with the onslaught of AIDS, many of us by now have seen our friends as well as our parents suffer bad, distorted, technological deaths at the end of tubes and machines. Those nurses (and other healthcare providers) who have witnessed many of these deaths regularly often say: "Life's a bitch and then you die. If you're *lucky*." If you're not, you end up in ICU on a respirator.

We swear not to let that happen to ourselves or our loved ones when the time comes, but few of us actually do anything about it to assure our wishes will be met. If we're serious about what we want, we need to tell whomever will be making our decisions when we can no longer do so, and to legally empower them to follow our wishes, with such advanced directives as a Living Will and a Durable Power of Attorney for Healthcare.

Because I regularly help people fill out these forms, I have personally had both documents for years. The advantage of working in a hospital, in addition to providing daily reminders of the fragility of life, is that we all know what to do if any of us comes into the Emergency Room or Intensive Care Unit in bad shape. We have all taken solemn oaths not to do to each other what we are ordered to do to most of the people in there - prolong their existence (not life) and extend their dying.

As I talk with people (of all age groups) around the country, there is a strong interest in exercising more control over the way we die, both when and how. Indeed, there is much discussion about the concept of a GOOD DEATH.

For the last few years I have asked groups to write down three characteristics of a Good Death for themselves. Regardless of whether they are counselors, elderly, long term care workers, nurses, clergy, nutritionists, or business workers, by far the most commonly reported requirements are QUICK, PAINLESS, and AT HOME. It is interesting that those are the exact antitheses of PROTRACTED, PAINFUL, and IN THE HOSPITAL, which is where eighty-five percent of deaths occur with high-tech accompaniment.

The next most reported are NOT ALONE, ASLEEP, and NO SUFFERING. In church groups I've addressed, everybody wants to go to heaven, but nobody wants to die to get there. There is a small connection they have missed.

I have collected some unusual answers to my informal GOOD DEATH query, with no seeming correlation to the particular group, except that nurses always want to die CONTINENT (with bowel and bladder control.) Creative responses have come from all groups across age, sex and occupation lines. Some of them are:

AFTER SEX. Not many people will readily blurt this one out, though if I ask for hands most people (frequently Episcopalians) will admit to thinking it. Some will clean it up by saying DOING SOMETHING FUN. Texans, in their polite Southern way, want to die IN THE SADDLE. (Yippie ki-yaaaaaa. Thud.) One person added WITH CHOCOLATE. AND NEW BATTERIES IN MY VIBRATOR.

GRINNING. SMILING. LOOKING GOOD. These people (often men) want everyone to know they've had a satisfied life, or death, or that they know something now that they'll never, ever tell you and they get the last smirk, so there. They also want to be shown to be sartorially correct to the end, as if their picture in the casket could adorn the cover of GQ or ELLE.

PUBLIC. EXCITING. DRAMATIC. No introverts here, or maybe people who have been so introverted their whole lives that they want to go out in a blaze of something or other. Watch for them on the nightly news, or being posthumously interviewed by Oprah.

SAYING SOMETHING RELEVANT. This is the Gertrude Stein line. ("But Alice, what was the question?") These people want to be remembered for their final comments, but seldom are. To really pull this one off you have to die drug free and have lots of preparation time. I am often asked if people say meaningful things on their deathbeds. The answer is no. Most people just gurgle their way into oblivion. But my favorite line was from a young woman whose husband had just been out with his friends having a quick dinner. Her final words were: "You smell like a garlic pizza."

Other definitions of a GOOD DEATH have included: IN THE NETHERLANDS; WITH ONE LAST CHANCE TO HAVE MEXICAN FOOD; NOT IN AN AIRPLANE; and FEBRUARY 29TH SO MY FAMILY WOULD ONLY HAVE TO REMEMBER THE DATE EVERY FOUR YEARS.

The comment about the Netherlands is telling. It is public knowledge that the Dutch are the only people to have five legal criteria for active, voluntary euthanasia:

1. You must be dying. (One of the better criteria.)

2. You must make the request yourself. (Another good one, especially if you're the rich parent.)

3. You must make the request over time, to assure your seriousness. (You can't spend the night on the town, wake the next morning feeling like hell and demand to be killed.)

4. You must be in *intractable suffering*. Suffering that can only be relieved by death. (I'll come back to that.)

5. It must be done by a physician. (So it isn't botched.)

For me, and for many of us at this stage of life, the most important criterion is number four. We don't want to suffer or cause suffering to others. But we will have to learn to differentiate between *pain* and *suffering*, which most people pronounce as one word.

There is no good reason to die in pain. Given the numerous kinds and combinations of narcotic and other medications available to relieve discomfort, it is not necessary or required to experience it. In fact, when the Dutch discuss "intractable suffering," they are not talking about pain. They know that it can and should be quelled and are not narco-weenies (like we are) about doing so.

So the question is, if *suffering* isn't *pain*, what is it? We will have to redefine the meaning of the word to include the suffering of indignity, of humiliation, denigration, helplessness, loss of personhood, the sense of no longer being who you were, the suffering of dependence, and the suffering of the soul. And we will have to ask why we cannot quell that kind of suffering as well as physical pain?

In our search for a good death we will have to address the issues of euthanasia and assisted suicide. Neither should be an option until everyone has a right to healthcare, because money will be an issue. If you are dying and have no health insurance, euthanasia/assisted suicide may look like a reasonable way out. If you have insurance but will deplete your account and your kids or grandkids college education in the process, euthanasia and assisted suicide may look equally acceptable. Both are end runs around a healthcare system that requires high tech death.

But we will have national healthcare, or something very like it. And we will have to decide how to allow assisted suicide and active voluntary euthanasia as logical, caring alternatives to prolonged suffering for those who choose them.

If my wife dies before I do, I probably would not marry again; not that there would be anyone crazy enough to get in line. But who knows? She may well be the one making the decision and not me. And if I am dying, I expect her to honor my wishes to maintain control over that process. At least from this age in the game, the thought of Alzheimer's or ALS (Lou

Gehrig's Disease) or some other slow, wasting or debilitated death is not consistent with who I am. I see nothing immoral or unethical about deciding to hasten an inevitable death to quell suffering (as defined by the dying person.) I fully expect to have the right either to do it or have it done.

Life is short and life is uncertain.

Death *is* certain, and we're going to be dead a long time. The key to a good death is a good life, well lived and well loved and well served, with as few regrets as possible.

Maybe the bumper stickers are right. Carpe Diem. Cave Canem. Illigitimi Non Carborundum. Caca Pasa. Besame Mucho.

But above all: Lighten Up. It's only death and life and death and life and death and life. Ad infinitum.

Eat dessert first.

EXERCISE

I am a runner.

I never thought those four words would come out of my mouth.

I was more than unathletic as a kid - I was gelatinous. In sixth grade I was a pyramid of baby-fat: thin arms, a tire around my middle, and humungous thighs.

In my elementary school we had gym class with the girls. We wore baggy shorts and they wore those blue one piece things that, if you were real quick you could see their panties, and they knew it because they could see up our shorts as well. That was what passed for sex education in 1957.

The turning point in my physical exertion career involved a mountain kid named Jimmy Oakes, probably because he looked like one (a mountain and an oak.) He was huge, but he was a nice boy. You can afford to be nice to people who can't possibly hurt you. Nobody could hurt Oakes. A Mac truck couldn't hurt Oakes. He had been in a couple of initial, beginning of the year fights to determine his standing in the sixth grade food chain and pulverized the opposition into immediate submission. My own fight had left me somewhere near the scrape line. I made Gumby look muscular.

Once when I went to the dreaded gym class for my daily dose of embarrassment, the morning's entertainment was to watch Jimmy Oakes out leg-wrestle everybody in the known universe, including cattle. (For those of you in Oklahoma, I made that last part up about the cattle.)

Leg wrestling involves lying on the floor side by side in opposite directions and lifting your right leg three times in the air. On the third count you hook the other person's leg and try to pull him over, thereby providing a lesson in sex education for all the girls who are looking up your pants, and giggling.

"I'll try it," I said, after Oakes had sufficiently creamed all the other boys and even the fat girls with legs like telephone poles. I was pissed that the stupid gym teacher thought me so unworthy as to not put me in line to get killed.

Kids didn't know whether to laugh or yawn. They did both. Half left to have extra time to get out of their smelly gym clothes and into their smelly school clothes. The remaining boys stood around and told jokes or tried to catch the girls unbuttoning on the way to their locker room. So only the fast dressers and those who wanted to see Oakes do it one more time were left to watch the anticipated slaughter.

The gym teacher called the numbers. On the third call, I hooked Oakes' ankle and pulled him over on top of me. With thighs like mine I could have toppled the Empire State Building.

Nobody moved.

The gym teacher looked at me like I cheated.

"Again," Oakes grumbled.

One. Two. Three. Over he came.

A crowd gathered. People came from both locker rooms, in various states of undress. Sex education was at its maximum.

"Best of five," Oakes whispered.

I lost on three and five but won on four, so I won the set. Jimmy Oakes and I became fast friends and nobody ever messed with either of us, for different reasons. I also decided that, someday, I could possibly do something with my body besides feed it.

In the eighth grade my best friend and I, after much deliberation, figured that going out for track would make us look macho for the girls. We went to the first practice to run cross country. Neither of us recovered in time to go to the second practice.

In high school I magically dropped the fat and attained the weight and body size I have had ever since. But, even in college, I declined every opportunity to exercise, only going to the gym to do the required two years of Health, Physical Education, Recreation which those of us who hated it called HYPER because of the hyper teacher who loathed the grubs in the class and rejoiced in our inability to run a mile. At least we didn't have class with women, though by then the sex education would have been better.

As I hit my early thirties the running craze got a jock lock on America. Everybody I worked with was running. Of course, I worked at a Texas jail where the "running group" the marathoner nurse led for inmates was highly suspect by the guards, except Old Bill. He just sat his 210 lbs in his red pickup, his shotgun perched on his lap and said: "That's okay, son. They cain't outrun this."

I didn't get the running thing. As I sat at Deep Eddy swimming pool and watched all the various sizes and shapes of runners on the trail I wondered why anyone in their right mind would strip down to skimpy shorts and purposely go out to hurt themselves. I joked that I'd take up running when I saw someone doing it with a smile on his face.

After my wife died it was either running or suicide. I decided to try running first. It was a tie for which was worse. But the more I ran, the more I liked it. It was something I could do solo, with only myself to compete against. It took up the vast amount of alone time I had, it used up a lot of energy, and it proved to offset anything I ate or drank. I came to realize then that if I ran three times a week I could eat or drink anything. And in those days I did.

My forties changed all that. I can't drink like I did before and still have a good day following. There must be some turn in the road of your liver at age forty that forever ends the ability to drink volumes of alcohol, metabolize it immediately and start the next day fresh as if it never happened. Now when I have more than two drinks in the evening, my brain reminds me of it in the morning - for hours - even with coffee. Optimists and health freaks would say that is a change toward the healthier. I still prefer to believe, with the French, that a daily glass of red wine increases lifespan. Besides, as Redd Foxx said: "Twenty years from now all those health food freaks are gonna feel real stupid, lyin' in the hospital, dyin' of nothin'."

Surprisingly, my over-forty body responded to running like it had been twiddling its muscles waiting around for me to catch on since the Jimmy Oakes incident. I did the 5K races in the tiny Texas towns of Schwertner, Dime Box, Marble Falls, Round Rock and LaGrange. By forty-two I had graduated to 10Ks, and began to sense that the inevitable marathon was lurking just around the corner. I got on a schedule and worked out at the hospital fitness center, distracting as it was due to the variously attired women.

The dress code eluded me. They wore mid-calf leg tights under bike pants under wind shorts. All three articles of clothing were different but colors were carefully matched and coordinated with their tight fitting sport bras bobbing beneath their off-the-shoulder designer tank tops. How did they do this? *Why* did they do this? Who cared what you looked like when you exercised? Obviously the men didn't. At their various fitness machines, the men looked like a drawer of mismatched sox. If it passed the sniff test, you put it on. You were going to sweat in it anyway. The women looked like a brand new box of Neon Crayolas.

You could also tell these carefully attired women (and, to be fair, some of the men) were under forty because they talked as they exercised. The rest of us were there sweating our brains out and desiring nothing more than to be ignored while we did it, which is why we all wore headsets tuned to oldies stations. Plus our aging lungs wouldn't let us talk and sweat at the same time.

The women my age wore grays and blacks, with white baggy t-shirts down to their knees, like choir vestments for the Singing Runs. As reluctant as they were to call attention to their bodies, they were not at all afraid to show their sweat. The under-forty women only perspired from the neck down. No innocent sweat bead, however persistent, could possibly penetrate the mask of makeup plastered over their pores. I wondered what would happen if sweat built up beneath that cemented surface like steam in an unvented pressure cooker and suddenly, without warning, exploded, sending Max Factor shards flying through the room impaling innocent exercisers with deadly cosmetic shrapnel? It gave new meaning to the phrase "blonde bombshell."

Despite the entertainment, I trained for and eventually ran the Austin Marathon. I wanted to come in under six hours. I did it in five hours, fifty eight minutes and fifty nine seconds. As I crossed the finish line, I respectfully requested my family to shoot me if I ever brought up the subject again.

I did and they didn't. It must be like having a baby. By the time you're ready for the next one you've forgotten the horror of birthing the first.

But that can't be the whole story, at least not for those of us in our forties. Indeed, there is something about being in your mid-forties that makes running a marathon more tempting, even enticing. Not many of your peers can do it. It must validate that you're not dead yet and that what you may lack in speed you make up in endurance. Even Freud could figure that one out.

Two years later enough time had elapsed for my brain to romanticize the first one, and I began to think about doing another marathon. Going through my runner's magazine, I watched for just the right race - and found it.

What I told myself was that it sounded exotic. And I like alliteration. That's why I chose the Maui Marathon. I also thought it was flat.

I started training on my forty-sixth birthday in October for the March run. Back at the hospital fitness center my coach, Joy, herself a marathoner, supported all my typical runner's beliefs, the things that made training sound logical:

Anyone can run 26 miles.
If you run 13 you can run 26.

You deal with muscle pain by running it off.
All knee problems will vanish by race day.
The goal is to make it to the *starting* line
  - *uninjured.*

Three weeks before the race I developed muscle problems in my knees and quads. I was worried I wouldn't make it to the starting line. Joy assured me I would. But she's as crazy as I am. We would both run a race with gangrenous extremities if necessary.

The next week a physician friend limped into the Intensive Care Unit where I was visiting patients, and I asked him about his injury. Runners develop great social skills from talking about every aspect of the sport, the most entertaining of which is "Gross Injuries," subcategory: "Feet." I told him about the upcoming Maui and he groaned. Another friend of his had run it and told him it was a horrendous race. "The last ten miles are uphill," he said. I knew this was an exaggeration, much as two other people had joked that they heard the course was "up a volcano."

The plane trip there was easy and I had a full day to carbo-load. I vacuumed everything I could see in a twenty-four hour period. It was great fun. My wife was astonished and my daughter thought I acted like every boy in her eighth grade class.

Sunday morning I woke at 4am, ate, dressed, lubed and drove to the opposite end of the island to the starting point. I had made it (relatively) uninjured, with minor knee pain. In the blackness of the

Maui morning, I checked in and was interviewed by a Japanese camera crew doing a documentary on the race. I pointed to my "Run For Your Oats" t-shirt from the Oatmeal Run in Bertram. "I'm from Austin, Texas," I said. "The Lone Star State." They nodded like I was from Mars, or possibly an asylum, and gave me a cup of coffee.

This was a small race. About 300 bleary eyed runners were there. That should have been my first clue that perhaps the word was out on this thing.

My second clue that trouble lay ahead was when the Reverend Muggahoonawongabonga of the "Little Church to the Right of Attila the Hun" stood to lead us in a politically incorrect prayer that excluded everyone of Buddhist, Moslem, Confucian, Taoist, and Jewish faiths, which meant about 297 of the runners. Already I felt special.

The third clue came just before the starting shout (no gun, no horn, no loud speaker). It was when the race director announced, with Tammy Faye sobs, that the race was being dedicated to "Old Gimpy" Henderson, who had actually "UP AND DIED" during last year's race. (I am not making this up.)

Shout. We're off.

I had no time to ponder the starting fiasco. I was concentrating too hard on where the heck I was going. It was pitch black out there and we were given strict instructions to "stay to the left of the FLARES" or we'd be disqualified. By whom? Bats?

In seconds I was entirely alone at the rear with

the fading flares, inhaling billows of red burning sulfur dioxide with 25.2 miles to go. At Mile 2 the coffee from the Japanese camera crew suddenly wanted out. I looked for a pit stop. A porta-potty.

There were none. And there were none the entire race. Where did they think all that carbo-loading was going to unload? Fortunately, Hawaiian tourist literature had accurately described the lush vegetation of the island, and it was behind this that I improvised.

The morning was cool. I had gotten rid of the rented coffee for which I had served as brief middle man, and was on my way to a personal marathon record, feeling great, fulfilling a dream, running in Maui - in the wind and the rain.

The Trade Winds arrived that morning doing 30MPH, and the omnipresent mist caught a ride on it. The Winds blew from behind to urge me on. The mist cooled. The sun broke through the clouds over the volcano to the west while the misty eastern mountains glowed green and white - and a huge rainbow emerged with colors so vivid they were tangible.

It was Paradise. Nirvana. I had died and gone to Heaven. Best run anywhere, any time in my life. Visual, physical, mental, spiritual ecstacy. Superlatives understate the experience. It couldn't possibly get any better than this.

At Mile 8 I had "a little knee problem." I blew a cylinder or popped a gasket, technical terms for a loud crunch in the right kneecap. But there was the wind and the mist and the rainbow and the wonderfully FLAT terrain and then - another incredible rainbow. It was as if they propped them up on cue, Disney-like, at appropriate times when you needed them. I couldn't quit now and end this experience. So I stopped, stretched, slowed my pace and figured I only had eighteen more to go.

Having crossed the island, the course now headed over what was described in the race packet as the "gently rolling highway" of the coast. This is Hawaiian for "up and down big hills on the shoulder of a two lane truck racetrack." With gravel.

After the fourth "hill" I hit Mile 11 depleted of fluids. Water had been offered every two miles from Mile 6 - but no electrolytes. I missed the efficiency of the Austin race with funny people doing encouraging things to make you think you were nearly at the finish line at each stop.

Whether it was fluid hallucination or Hawaii being Hawaii, I looked up ahead and found an even more beautiful rainbow beckoning me on. Off to my left was the ocean with miles of whitecaps, whales somewhere just beneath the water, wind still cooling and sun warming me. I was back in Paradise and ready to go to the end - when the ultimate high occurred.

My headset blared out the theme song from *Hawaii 5-0*.

I saw the wave, flashed scenes from the t.v. show of my kid-hood, and mouthed the immortal words of McGarrett: "Book 'em, Danno. Murder One." It was too good. No one deserved this much pleasure. If I died at Mile 12 my life would be complete.

At Mile 13 I wished I had.

Everything changed. Reversed. The wind switched direction and now came towards me at 30MPH. The mist was replaced by unrelenting heat. The course veered off the main paved highway with the ocean view and the rainbows onto the old, seldom used, broken rock and dirt, sugar cane plantation road where they filmed World War III movies. Barren, wasteland, after-the-radiation scenes.

Some things remained the same. There were still no porta-pits, and no electrolytes every two miles. I got worried. I was getting a little dizzy, my knee hurt and my quads were screaming, there was nobody in sight except the sixty year old man about a half mile ahead of me I'd been following for the last hour. The four gazillion carbo-cals I'd eaten the night before were digested and ready for recycling.

I didn't like this. What was a forty-six year old person doing out here, anyway? What if I collapsed? Who would find me? Boarding the return flight at the airport my wife and daughter would just think the race was taking me longer than usual. I'd come home, they'd think. As they took off perhaps they would see the buzzards and think: No, it couldn't be. Not our Dad. He'll finish the race. Eventually.

At least it couldn't get worse.

Wrong. At Mile 16, after I had been repeatedly

whacked on the head by sugar cane as I squatted in the middle of a field for a pit stop, the Curse of the ICU Doctor came true. The road indeed began to go UP HILL. I began to look for a grave marker. This must have been where "Old Gimpy" bought it.

By Mile 20 I walked more than ran. At Mile 23 the course led through an abandoned sugar cane factory that looked like a set from a mass murder movie. At Mile 25, racewalking, I smoked the sixty year old guy.

Of course I ran the last half mile for show, crossed the finish line at 5 hours 31 minutes, and embraced my wife and daughter who had a beer and a camera waiting, in that order.

Monday I couldn't do stairs. Tuesday I could go up but not down. "Wednesday I got better just for spite." Thursday I ran two miles on the beach before we headed for the airport and home, where Debi got me a t-shirt saying: "Friends don't let friends run marathons."

A few months post race, when the five toenails grew back and I could run four miles without pain, I started thinking. The Austin Marathon course was hilly and difficult. The Maui Marathon was a Heaven and Hell race; had they reversed the course my time would have been far more reasonable. So the only possible conclusion from the run is that I need to find a *flat* one, or the one in Burgundy, France, where you run through fifty vineyards, with wine tasting and oyster bars along the way.

My wife subtly slipped a brochure in my running bag for Marathoners Anonymous. ("Hi. I'm Chuck M., and I run.") In "M.A." you get a buddy and, when you get the urge to do a marathon, you call him up and have a drink until it passes. In the meantime, I'm looking for a marathon with great alliteration. A flat one.

I continue to run. I tell myself it will lengthen my life and keep me fit as I nudge closer to fifty. I like to sweat. I like to run in the Austin heat and then jump into a cold pool. I like still being able to eat what I want and drink a few non-alcoholic beers as long as I run three times a week. So I'll keep running until I can't, with one more marathon before the big 5-0 that is not Hawaiian.

I have noticed that people in their late forties often end up on bicycles. If my knees ever quit I suppose I will have to do that. In the meantime, my current goal is to die of a heart attack after I win my age category in a 10K at 103. Or die making love celebrating it.

EPILOGUE

What have my forties taught me so far? If I had to distill it down to a few sentences, what would they be?

As it turns out, I was asked to do exactly that by a couple of friends who were holding a graduation brunch for twenty-five high school seniors. I first came up with ten things, then twelve, then fifteen. That seemed like a good place to stop.

So here they are, as addressed to high school graduates, but possibly relevant for the rest of us wading knee deep through the murky waters of mid-life. It may be that we only discover what we have learned when we pass it along to our kids.

15 Things I Wish My Mother, Father or Anybody Had Told Me

Some of these will be surprising to you, some obscure, and others unbelievable for the present time. Some your parents will like and you will not, others you will like and your parents will not. Some you both may not be too crazy about. But all are true, and may help to carry you through difficult decisions at critical moments.

1. DEATH HAPPENS - Let's take the biggie first. The death rate on planet Earth is 100%. One out of one dies. And death is no respecter of age or convenience. Infants die. Adolescents die. Young *and* old people die. You need not be morbidly preoccupied by these facts, but you also need not be too surprised when accident, injury or terminal illness hits close to home, if it hasn't already.

Nobody knows what happens when we die, despite what they say in popular books and on Oprah. A large proportion of people in the world think we "go on" to Somewhere. Lots of people think we "come back" to finish things. You will need to decide what you think about this and live accordingly. The most important thing about death is to know it is inevitable, that we ought not to prolong it unnecessarily with machines, and that, as a dying cancer patient told me: "Whether I'm here or there I'm okay, 'cause either place I'm loved."

Eighty-five percent of deaths in the U.S. occur in healthcare settings (hospitals, nursing homes, rehabilitation centers). That means there is an eighty-five percent chance someone else will decide when and how you will die. It might, therefore, be a good idea to talk with your parents, best friend, teacher, or clergy about what you might want - or not want - done to you if you suddenly became incapacitated, comatose or severely disabled. If your state has such a form, fill out a Living Will to make certain you have "clear and convincing evidence" of your

wishes, including organ donation. Many people who
have not yet come to some terms with death spend
their whole lives worrying about it - and forget to
live. Once you've done your Living Will - reread
number 15.

2. THINK AND TAKE CHANCES - There was a
sign in the construction area of St. David's Hospital
where I work that said THINK - TAKE NO
CHANCES. It is a message that most parents would
like indelibly branded on the brain of their teenager,
supposedly to protect and keep you from trouble
and harm. But the truth is that not one successful
adult got to where he/she is today by taking no
chances. We all ignored the pleading from our parents and took a chance: moved, bought a house, fell
in love, changed jobs, travelled, broke up a relationship, had a child, got something we really wanted,
gave up a child, helped someone else at great cost to
ourselves, let someone help us, healed a hurt. Everybody remembers that Babe Ruth held the home run
record - but nobody remembers that he also holds
the record for the number of times *striking out* - and
that there's a direct correlation between the two.

Now this does not mean taking stupid chances
for mindless reasons, or being irresponsible for your
or another's emotional or physical safety. But it *does*
mean being open to ideas, places, people and experiences different from what you've known. It does
mean being a little outrageous from time to time and
not necessarily always conforming to your peer

group's way of seeing things.

The Apostle Paul (among many others) said not to be conformed to this world, but to be transformed by the renewal of your spirit - a spirit that urges us to take risks. Life is too short not to - and there are too many problems to be solved to waste time repeating the mistakes of your elders.

3. YOU'VE ONLY GOT ONE BODY - Even though we often feel like it, we're not invulnerable or immortal. Old people say: "If I'd known my body was gonna last this long, I'd have taken better care of it." Your body has to last you a long time. What you do with it now can determine how long it lasts, what systems eventually break down, and what kind of quality of life you have in the meantime.

Nearly two-thirds of the deaths in America are the result of four conditions: cardiac disease, cancer, traumatic injuries, and strokes. A large percentage of those conditions could be reduced or avoided if we paid attention to our diet, took time to drive defensively and safely, exercised regularly, and quit smoking. AIDS is the second leading cause of death in the 25-44 year old age group and the fifth leading over all cause of death in the US. Over one fifth of AIDS patients got infected in their teens. Simply put: wear helmets, seat belts, and condoms, but not at the same time.

You've only got seventy or eighty more years on the planet and one body in which to spend the entire time. Think of it as getting the only car you can ever own for the rest of your life at age 20, and take care of it accordingly.

4. GIVE SOMETHING BACK - At the penitentiary where I worked the inmates said "What goes around comes around." Jesus said "The measure you give will be the measure you get." The truth is that none of us got to where we are today entirely on our own. All of us, adults and adolescents alike, relied on the efforts of someone else, our families and religious groups, the volunteer help of people in the community putting in extra hours of work, donating time and money and talent to the school and the education system, to city boards and commissions.

You may not be able to do this at first, but please remember your obligation to give back some of what you've been given. There is so much suffering in the world that simply cannot and will not be alleviated by official organizations spending money. If suffering is to be relieved it will only be at the individual, one on one level, by each one of us volunteering time, going out of our way to help, developing creative solutions to heal the sick, clothe the homeless, feed the poor, and comfort the dying.

Be reminded of this every time you read the warning on each can or bottle of soda you pick up: *No deposit. No return.*

5. QUESTION EVERYTHING - THEN TELL THE TRUTH - From the time you first set foot outside school with diploma in hand there will be people

telling you what is right and what you must do to
succeed and what kind of car you must drive and
which deodorant you have to use and which tooth-
paste will guarantee success and which lies you'll
have to tell to get ahead and exactly how the system
works and why and how you can get around all of
that the easy way.

When confronted with these situations, don't believe everything you see, hear, or feel (especially feelings - they come and go faster than anything else).
Paul (Apostle and McCartney) says "Question everything, and hold fast to what is good." Question
everything, and run for cover when anyone says
"We've always done it this way." Now it may be
that we've always done it this way for a very good
reason, but at least get an explanation of that reason,
and decide if it still makes good sense.

Then, even though it is sometimes difficult and
will continue to be unpopular, TELL THE TRUTH
about your opinions, your feelings, your actions and
your beliefs. It's a lot easier to remember the truth
than to remember the lies we've told and get them
straight to different people. More importantly, if the
people around you can't handle the truth, then you
need to be around different people.

**6. WE DO TO OTHERS WHAT WE WANT
DONE TO OURSELVES** - Contrary to everything
you've heard, The Golden Rule is not about what we
should do, it is about what we *do* do. We basically

treat other people the way we believe we should be treated.

This is an important thing to remember when examining the behavior of other people - bosses, teachers, parents, siblings, significant others. If we view what they do as an indication of how they see themselves we can be less judgmental about them. If we view our own behavior using this guideline, we can get some insight into our motivation and possibly change the way we do things.

Now it is important also to realize that, regardless how well we treat others, there is no guarantee that we will get treated well in return. Life is conspicuously unfair. We do not get what we deserve, or deserve what we get. We get a lot of undeserved suffering *and* a lot of undeserved joy, and there is no correlation between what we get and what kind of person we are. But just because life is unfair does not give us permission to be unfair in return. We must continue to be fair in the very face of unfairness, to be just in the face of injustice, to be honest in the face of dishonesty. Only by doing so will we ultimately treat others as we wish to be treated.

7. WE OFTEN CHOOSE MATES TO WORK OUT UNFINISHED BUSINESS WITH PARENTS - AND IT NEVER WORKS OUT - There are at least two theories on this at the present time. The first is that we tend to choose a mate that reminds us of the parent of the opposite sex. Whether we have had a good or awful relationship with that parent doesn't matter. In either case, we believe we can "change" the partner to be the better model (even perfect model) of that parent. What we do not realize is that the mate is doing the exact same thing with us, and when our hidden agendas break down, so do the relationships.

The second theory is that, although we tend to choose a mate based on our idealized image of the parent of the opposite sex, that is a good thing because it gives us the opportunity to work out unfinished business with that parent through the relationship with the mate - assuming the mate and the relationship are hardy enough to maintain that kind of working through. Once done, in therapy or in the daily working out of partner relations, we are supposed to be further along in our psychological maturity.

Which of these theories is true is up for debate. For now, it is enough to be aware of how we make choices concerning partners and eventually mates, to realize that we cannot really "change" anyone but ourselves, and to ask ourselves carefully how it is that we are attracted to this other person, what we expect from him/her and from ourselves. With the divorce rate hovering at 52%, such self examination could save a lot of pain.

8. LISTEN FOR THE SOUND OF GOD'S LAUGHTER. - Contrary to what you'll hear from most people who claim to be religious - *nobody's perfect*. In fact, perfection is not even the goal. What *is* the goal? According to the prophet Micah it's to "...do justice, love mercy and walk humbly with God." What we are called to do first of all is to forgive one another - and ourselves - when we make the many mistakes that are in our future (and our past); we are to treat one another with justice and fairness in all of our interactions; and our walking humbly with God may mean standing up firmly before others for what we believe, especially when it is unpopular or contrary to the way peer pressure or society demands.

And the only way to do all of this is to listen for the sound of God's laughter. You will hear it in the heat of arguments and in the heat of passion, when things look their worst as well as when things are at their best, when you are feeling most down and hopeless and when you are on top of the world, when everything is falling apart or coming together, and sometimes even when you look in the mirror in the morning to shave your face or do your hair. It is that sound in the background that puts everything back in perspective, that defuses shame and defeats evil; indeed it is God's laughter that joins in our successes and breaks through our failures, reminding us constantly that we are loved and accepted and forgiven regardless of whether we succeed or fail.

Listen for the sound of God's laughter. If you haven't heard it yet, you will. And don't worry about finding God. God will find you when you are ready.

9. WHAT GOES AROUND, COMES AROUND - This simple law of the universe, when remembered, will keep you out of more trouble than anything else. If I lie, cheat, steal, I fully expect the same will be done to me. If someone wrongs me, I expect that person will be wronged - but not by me. The universe will see to it, guaranteed, even though I may never know about it.

The other behavior affected by this truth is the old "to get a friend, be a friend" number. Real friendships (some of which will last a lifetime) require constant nurturing and regular attention. They cannot be taken for granted. If they are, they will not be there when you need them. The only way to endure the hardships and successes of life ahead of you is with the ever present support of close friends: friends to talk to and confide in, friends to hold and be held by, friends to laugh with, friends to remind us who we are, and who we once were.

10. VOTE OR SHUT UP - Americans stay away from the voting booths in greater numbers than any other democracy - and then complain about our elected officials. That's screwy. If you care about the way your city or county or state (or nation) is run, take the time to vote. If you don't care how high your taxes are, how good your schools are, whether you have safe streets and clean air, then don't vote - but don't complain when decisions are made for you by people you didn't bother to elect. Either you are part of the solution, or you're part of the problem. You choose.

11. SEX IS EXCITING, FUN AND DANGEROUS - Our bodies are great resources of pleasure, excitement and fun. Expressing our sexuality means being vulnerable, risking our feelings, becoming comfortable with our physical and emotional self. We are able to experience great depths of passion, infatuation, attraction, and love. Along with these feelings come the obvious dangers of hurt, disappointment, disillusionment, and rejection.

The important factor here is balance. It is important to be aware of the physical risk involved in sexual activity. The rate of sexually transmitted disease in the US increased dramatically in the last five years, especially syphilis, gonorrhea, chlamydia, and other illnesses that can cause permanent damage, sterility, or the inability to carry a fetus to term. The problems of AIDS and unwanted pregnancy are obvious.

There is no such thing as "safe sex." That's an oxymoron. Sex is never safe, physically or emotionally, and that's exactly why there's so much attention to it in society, advertising, and media. There is such a thing as responsible behavior, minimizing known risks, taking disease prevention seriously, and thoroughly enjoying the powerful feelings that sexual expression invokes. Don't feel pressured, and, when you're ready, proceed with caution.

12. EXPECT THE UNEXPECTED - The only thing you can count on is change. According to experts, you are likely to have to learn new job skills at least three times in your working career. Just when you think you understand something, the answers (or worse, the questions) will change. My generation thought we would live forever under the threat of nuclear war with the Soviet Union and that the Berlin Wall would always be there. You will have your own myths that will surprise you by changing, not always for the better. Be prepared for change by welcoming it and by not holding too tightly or defensively onto your stereotypes about who you are, who others are, and the way the world is.

But don't expect technology to save you, either. While we are making incredible technological advances in science and medicine and even in geopolitical structures, these advances may be as dangerous as they are helpful. Remember that the Chinese word picture for "crisis" is made up of two figures: one for danger and the other for opportunity. Welcome the future, and examine it carefully and thoroughly.

13. PERSISTENCE PAYS OFF - There's a story in the New Testament about a widow who so pesters a judge that he finally grants her petition just to get her out of his hair. If you want something enough, you will persist until you get it. If you believe in something enough, you will persist until it becomes reality. Remember that Gone With The Wind was rejected by publishers thirty two times and that The

Wizard of Oz had to be self published by the author because nobody thought it would sell.

Also remember to be careful what you ask for - you may get it and then face consequences you never imagined. Many people want fame and fortune and are ruined once either or both appear. Others want positions of responsibility and then are shocked to find themselves leading others into difficult areas of decision making they never imagined. Still others want to follow a dream but get themselves side-tracked by quick or easy successes, then give up the very dream that guided them.

Stick to your dreams and make them happen. Persist, persist, persist. The future of the planet depends on you.

14. LOVE DOESN'T LAST - COMMITMENT DOES - Somewhere we learn from the popular culture - romance stories, records, poetry, soap operas, movies - that love holds everything together in a relationship. That is a lie, and you'll do well to know it now. The truth is that love, like other feelings - passion, anger, despair, joy - is a fleeting feeling. It comes and goes. If your relationship is at the mercy of your feelings of love for each other then it will be bumpy indeed and ultimately not endure.

In fact, Larry Bugen, Ph.D. (author of Love and Renewal) says that *disillusionment* is a necessary part of every relationship, usually following close on the heels of romantic love. The function of romantic love is to get us attracted to each other. Once attracted and "in love", there is a normal period of *disillusionment* during which the couple sees each others warts and burps and bad smells and unpleasant characteristics that suddenly could not possibly be in line with the person we thought they were. How this period is handled can result in the breakup of the relationship or in moving further on into mature and lasting involvement.

In any case, it is not love that sustains a marriage or other committed relationship - it is the commitment that sustains the love, and that carries on even when feelings are obscured by work, children, illness, or disappointment. This is a difficult lesson to learn. Knowing it is true may ease its acceptance.

15. ENJOY THE JOURNEY - NOT JUST THE GOAL - Many people mistakenly imagine that they will be successful *"when..."* some event occurs, that they will take time to spend with their loved ones or family *"after..."* some goal is reached, that they will be happy *"if only..."* some specific thing would happen. These people get to the end of their lives never having lived.

The thing I hear most from survivors who have just had a loved one die is: "Gee, I wish we would have _____." Regrets are impossible to do over and get right a second time. It is important to live as much of a *regret free* life as you can. Keep your friends and loved ones up to date on how you feel about them. Keep yourself involved with the present journey, the task you are doing, the time you are spending *now*, because this time will never be here again. Tomorrow is not guaranteed, yesterday is over; the only time we really know we have together is right now.

Reread #1. And have a good life.

As I reviewed these fifteen things, I wondered if my life would have been different had I known them before forty? Could I have heard them before now or understood them? Would I have discounted them as worn-out advice to keep me in line, to prohibit the very experiences that led to these bits of wisdom?

If so, perhaps the fifteen things are less appealing as suggestions to young people and more effective as mid-course corrections for the fortysomething crowd. The plateau of mid-life is either a fortunate opportunity to exercise choice, or a genetically programmed circumstance forcing decisions. In either case, it is a time to reflect on where we've been in order to confirm, to continue and, most importantly, to adjust who we are and where we're going.

May these mid-life tales prove worthwhile in that effort.

Thanks for reading them.

See you at fifty.

Books by Chuck Meyer

Surviving Death: A Practical Guide to Caring for the Dying and Bereaved. 23rd Publications, Mystic, Connecticut, 1988, Second Edition, 1991. ($9.95) - A book for caregivers of the dying, for those who have experienced the death of a close loved one, and for those who themselves are dying. Dr. Karl Slaikeu, author of *Up From The Ashes* says: "...the book is unsurpassed in its concrete, step-by-step instructions on everything from talking with dying and bereaved individuals to coping with the full range of emotions and demands that survivors face. The author's blend of humor and sensitivity is especially refreshing." Winner of the Violet Crown Award for best non-fiction book of 1991, Austin Writer's League. (175pp.)

God's Laughter and Other Heresies. Stone Angel Books, Austin, Texas, Second Edition 1992. ($9.95). The author guarantees that "the buying of this book will definitely increase your own personal chances of getting into heaven". If heaven is a place of joy, sadness, tears and laughter, then he is correct, for the book is filled with all of the above. In addition to humorous commentaries on "Babies," "Stress," and "Bible Misquotes," the Christmas stories of "A Donkey Named Glory," "The Fourth Wise Man," "Harold the Innkeeper," and "An Angel Named Bubba," make delightful reading to children. (238pp.)

The Eighth Day, Letters, Poems and Parables. Stone Angel Books, Austin, Texas 1991. ($8.95). The Eighth Day is the day after God finished making everything and rested. It is the time *after* the seventh day and *before* Jesus comes back. The Eighth Day is *now.* These "letters, poems and parables" retell Bible stories from the viewpoint of the characters themselves. The Widow's Story, The Lawyer's Confession, and The Paralytic's Point of View, vividly portray the feelings and thoughts of ordinary people encountering an ordinary Jesus with extraordinary results for the rest of their lives. (175pp.)

The Gospel According to Bubba. Stone Angel Books, Austin, Texas, 1992. ($9.95). A 250lb Texas angel named Bubba appeared at the author's front door with "inside" information from "The Boss" and one heck of a thirst. It was down hill from there. Bubba's (unsolicited) insights are as Lone Star as "fahr aints". He's got comments on everything from Genesis to Bethlehem, from Blue Bell to Shiner Bock. If you're a Texan (native or born again) you'll cotton to stories like Beach Blanket Bubba, Bubba at Deep Eddy, and Bubba at Dime Box - and you'll want to share him with your friends. (150pp.)

Fast, Funny, and Forty. (Tales of Mid-Life.) Stone Angel Books, Austin, Texas, 1994. ($9.95). If you wake up one day and the world looks different - you're in your forties. Formerly simple things take on new meaning as you plummet into mid-life. Run (or perhaps walk) with the author through the gauntlet of HAIRCUT, CARS, MASSAGE, DAUGHTER, and EXERCISE. These and other forties stories provide laughter and insight into our "second adolescence." Fun and nostalgic for those over forty. Good preparation for those approaching it. Great gift item. Bifocals not included. (152pp.)

Books may be purchased at your local bookstore or by using this form:

Stone Angel Books
PO Box 27392
Austin, Texas 78755-2392

Please send:

_____ *Surviving Death* ($9.95)	$ _____
_____ *God's Laughter* ($9.95)	_____
_____ *The Eighth Day* ($8.95)	_____
_____ *Gospel/Bubba* ($9.95)	_____
_____ *Fast/Funny/Forty* ($9.95)	_____

Texans add 8% tax.   _____

Postage/handling
    1 book/$1.25   _____
    2 books/$2.00   _____
    3 books/$3.00   _____
    4 books/FREE   _____

                TOTAL $ _____

Make check or Money Order payable to

Stone Angel Books

NAME _____

ADDRESS _____

CITY _____ STATE _____ ZIP _____

(Want books autographed? Indicate "to whom".)